Better Homes and Gardens®

Meat Stretcher
Cook Book

© Meredith Corporation, 1974. All Rights Reserved.
Printed in the United States of America. First Edition. First Printing.
Library of Congress Catalog Card Number: 73-10912
SBN: 696-00720-7

On the cover: A delicious way to stretch your meat-buying dollar and please your family is to serve tempting *Vegetable-Stuffed Steaks* (see recipe, page 35) for dinner.

Above: Try *Calico Salisbury Steaks* at your next barbecue. These beef patties are prepared on the grill and then topped with a delicious *Salisbury Sauce* (see recipes, page 32).

Contents

BETTER HOMES AND GARDENS BOOKS

Editorial Director: Don Dooley
Managing Editor: Malcolm E. Robinson   Art Director: John Berg
Asst. Managing Editor: Lawrence D. Clayton   Asst. Art Director: Randall Yontz
Food Editor: Nancy Morton
Senior Food Editor: Joyce Trollope
Associate Editors: Rosemary Corsiglia, Sharyl Heiken
Assistant Editors: Sandra Mapes, Catherine Penney, Elizabeth Strait
Designer: Harijs Priekulis

Our seal assures you that every recipe in *Meat Stretcher Cook Book* is endorsed by the Better Homes and Gardens Test Kitchen. Each recipe is tested for family appeal, practicality, and deliciousness.

Money-Saving Meat Know-How

Smart shoppers know that the best ways to save money on meat are to plan ahead, take advantage of meat bargains, and use recipes that make meat go further.

Begin meat stretching by knowing the difference between how much protein you need and what you like to eat. Even the most active people need only 5 ounces of cooked meat, or its equivalent, plus the protein from 2 glasses of milk a day. This means you can build nutritious meals with 2 ounces of protein per serving. The chart on the back cover will help you figure how much meat to buy for a given number of servings.

This book will show you how to make smaller meat servings that don't look skimpy, how to use protein substitutes such as cheese and eggs, and how to make your own meat-stretching mixes.

Make the most of economical country-style ribs by serving *Orange-Glazed Ribs* (see recipe, page 50). Garnish this attractive dish with quartered orange slices and pass additional glaze, if desired.

6

Money-saving basics

In today's market there is a vast array of meat in all shapes and sizes. The key to successful meat stretching is to recognize the bargains. Learn to identify meat cuts by bone shape because it tells you the tenderness of the cut (see chart below).

In general, you can identify the shoulder cuts by the blade bone and leg or arm cuts by the round bone. These cuts usually have a lower price tag because they are among the less tender cuts. Cook them by moist-heat methods such as braising or cooking in liquid.

The rib bone, T-bone, and wedge bone are from the loin area and cost more because they are more tender. Cook these cuts by dry-heat methods such as roasting or broiling. The pictures on the following pages illustrate the more economical beef and pork cuts. These photographs can help you identify unfamiliar meat cuts in the supermarket.

Save money on meat by planning your purchases carefully. Before you go to the market, know your family's tastes and the amount of storage space you have. Purchase only those meats you know you will use and have room to store. Also, know how much time you have for food preparation. Many of the less-tender meat cuts are economical if you have

time to braise them or cook them in liquid. Also, try to use some of the less familiar types of meat such as liver, heart, tongue, kidney, tripe, and other variety meats. They can be real buys. Finally, make sure that you know how many people you will be serving. Unused leftovers are costly. The Meat Stretcher Price Chart on page 11 will help you plan how much meat to buy.

Storing Meat

Proper storage is vital in making meat go further. For maximum quality, store most fresh meat at 36° to 40° F. for no longer than two days. However, you can refrigerate some of the larger cuts of meat such as roasts up to four days. If you wish to keep meat longer, freeze it immediately. Variety meats and ground or chopped meats are more perishable, so cook them within one or two days. Store canned hams and picnics in the refrigerator unless package directions indicate otherwise. And don't keep these smoked meats in the freezer for more than 60 days because their flavor deteriorates rapidly at freezer temperatures.

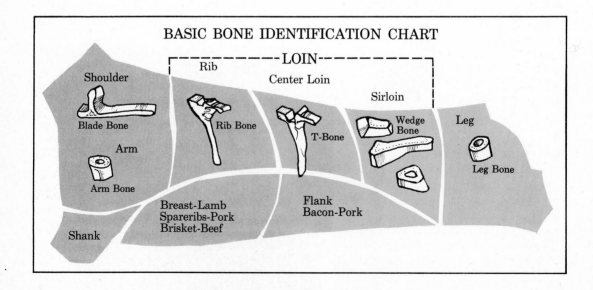

BASIC BONE IDENTIFICATION CHART

To store any leftover cooked meats, cool within two hours, wrap or cover them as soon as possible to prevent drying out, and store in the refrigerator. If you leave the meat in a large chunk, there will be less moisture loss. When storing meat with liquid or gravy, make sure, if possible, that the meat is completely covered by the liquid to prevent drying out.

There are also some things you need to keep in mind when freezing meat. Make sure the meat is fresh and in good condition. Prepare the meat before freezing by trimming off excess fat and cutting into serving-size portions when desirable. Don't salt the meat because this shortens freezer life. Wrap the meat in moisture-vaporproof wrapping material to keep as much air as possible sealed out and the moisture sealed in. Label meats with the name of the cut, the date, and the weight or number of servings. Freeze the meat at −10° F. or lower and keep it at 0° F. or below after it is completely frozen. And follow these freeze storage times:

Fresh beef . . . . 6 to 12 months
Fresh pork . . . . 3 to 6 months
Fresh lamb . . . . 6 to 9 months
Ground beef or lamb . . . . . 3 to 4 months
Ground pork . . . . 1 to 3 months
Variety meats . . . . 3 to 4 months

Preparing Meat

Help stretch meat by preparing it properly. Generally, meats can be divided into those best prepared by moist heat and those cooked best by dry heat. For the less-tender cuts, braising and cooking in liquid work best.

Braising: Brown the meat on all sides in a heavy pan. Pour off drippings. Season as desired. Add a small amount of liquid. Cover and cook at a low temperature till tender.

Cooking in liquid: Brown the meat on all sides in its own fat, if possible. Season. Cover the meat with liquid. Cover the kettle and simmer the meat till tender.

The large, tender cuts of meat should be roasted. Steaks, chops, and ground meat patties are best broiled or panfried.

Roasting: Season meat with salt and pepper, if desired. Place meat, fat side up, on a rack in a shallow roasting pan. Insert meat thermometer so it is centered in the thickest muscle. Roast at 300° to 350° till desired doneness. Do not add water or cover.

Broiling: Set oven regulator for broiling. Place meat on rack of broiler pan 2 to 5 inches from heat. Broil till topside is browned. Season with salt and pepper. Turn and cook till meat is desired doneness.

Panfrying: Brown the meat on both sides in a little fat. Season with salt and pepper. Cook at a moderate temperature, turning often till done. Do not cover meat.

Preventing excess shrinkage and cooking loss is important no matter what cooking method you use. The more cooking loss and shrinkage, the less usable meat there is. You can control cooking losses by making sure that you cook meat at a low temperature. Cook at a 325° oven temperature or use low heat on top of the range. Remember, the higher the cooking temperature, the greater the shrinkage will be. Also, cook meat to correct internal temperature (given in the recipe) to prevent drying out the meat.

Top: *Boneless Beef Round Rump Roast.* Bottom: *Bone-In Beef Round Rump Roast.* High-quality samples of these cuts can be roasted, but for assured tenderness, braise them.

Upper left: *Boneless Beef Chuck Pot Roast.* Lower left: *Beef Chuck Blade Pot Roast.* Lower right: *Beef Chuck Arm Pot Roast.* Braise these round- or blade-boned cuts.

Top: *Beef Round Tip Roast;* prepare by braising or roasting. Center: *Beef Bottom Round Steak;* braise or panfry. Bottom: *Beef Top Round Steak;* prepare by braising or panfrying.

Upper left: *Scored Beef Flank Steak.* Upper right: *Rolled Beef Flank Steak.* Bottom: *Beef Flank Steak Rolls.* All three cuts are the most tender when braised, but you can broil them.

Top: *Corned Boneless Beef Brisket;* cook in liquid. Lower left: *Beef Shank Cross Cuts;* braise or cook in liquid. Lower right: *Beef Plate Short Ribs;* braise or cook in liquid.

Top: *Beef Tongue.* Lower left: *Beef Sweet-breads.* Lower right: *Beef Kidney.* Variety meats can be used in many types of dishes, but be sure to cook them in liquid first.

Upper left: *Beef Tripe;* cook in liquid first, then panfry or broil. Upper right: *Beef Heart;* cook in liquid, then stuff and bake. Bottom: *Beef Liver;* panfry or cook in liquid.

Top: *Pork Shoulder Blade Roast;* roast. Lower left: *Smoked Pork Shoulder Roll;* roast or cook in liquid. Lower right: *Pork Shoulder Blade Steak;* either braise or panfry this cut.

Upper left: *Whole Smoked Pork Shoulder Picnic;* roast or cook in liquid. Lower left: *Canned Pork Shoulder Picnic;* roast. Lower right: *Smoked Pork Hocks;* roast or cook in liquid.

Upper left: Fully cooked *Smoked Ham; Shank Portion.* Upper right: *Rump Portion.* Both of the cuts can be roasted. Lower right: *Smoked Ham Center Slice;* broil, panfry, or roast.

Upper left: *Pork Loin Country-Style Ribs;* roast or braise. Upper right: *Pork Loin Back Ribs;* roast or braise. Bottom: *Pork Spareribs;* roast, braise, or cook this cut in liquid.

Comparing the Costs of Meats

Find the best meat buys by learning to use the Meat Stretcher Price Chart. This table helps you compare the cost per serving of meats ranging from $.49 to $2.59 per pound. The servings listed are based on approximately 2½ ounces of cooked meat each. Since the chart is designed to help you stretch meat, the portions may be smaller than you are accustomed to serving. You will want to weigh out a serving so you can become familiar with the size.

The meats listed in the chart are divided into three groups. The first group includes cuts that have no bone, those that have very little fat, and canned meats or fish. There will be some differences in shrinkage and cooking loss among the members of this group. The boneless beef and pork roasts, for example, will give slightly less cooked meat per pound than a boneless fully cooked ham. For the most part, however, plan on six servings to the pound for these meats.

The second group is made up of meat cuts with small bones, such as round steak and pork chops, and boneless cuts that have a higher fat content, such as smoked pork shoulder roll. Fresh fish and seafood are also part of this group. For meat-stretching recipes, you can get three servings per pound.

The final group includes meats with a high porportion of bone, such as poultry and beef or pork ribs, as well as cuts that are extremely fatty, such as bulk pork sausage. These cuts will not stretch as far so plan on only two servings to the pound.

Here's how the chart works. Run your finger across one of the rows. You'll find that ground beef at $.89 a pound works out to $.30 a serving. But a boneless beef roast at $1.69 a pound works out to just $.28 a serving. The chart tells you that even though boneless beef roast costs more per pound, it costs less per serving than ground beef.

For another example, suppose you are debating between buying beef round steak that sells for $1.49 a pound and country-style ribs on sale for $.89 a pound. The chart tells you that the country-style ribs are a better buy since they cost $.45 a serving while the round steak is $.50 a serving.

MEAT STRETCHER PRICE CHART

Price per pound	Cost per Serving of Boneless and Lean Meat (6 servings per pound)	Cost per Serving of Meat with Some Bone or Fat (3 servings per pound)	Cost per Serving of Meat with Much Bone or Fat (2 servings per pound)
$ .49	$ .08	$ .16	$ .25
.59	.10	.20	.30
.69	.12	.23	.35
.79	.13	.26	.40
.89	.15	.30	.45
.99	.17	.33	.50
1.09	.18	.36	.55
1.19	.20	.40	.60
1.29	.22	.43	.65
1.39	.23	.46	.70
1.49	.25	.50	.75
1.59	.27	.53	.80
1.69	.28	.56	.85
1.79	.30	.60	.90
1.89	.32	.63	.95
1.99	.33	.66	1.00
2.09	.35	.70	1.05
2.19	.37	.73	1.10
2.29	.38	.76	1.15
2.39	.40	.80	1.20
2.49	.42	.83	1.25
2.59	.43	.86	1.30
	Boneless Beef and Pork Roasts, Beef Flank Steak, Boneless Ham, Stew Meat, Liver, Heart, Tongue, Canadian-style Bacon, Frankfurters, Bologna, other Luncheon Meat, Canned Fish and Seafood	Round Steak, Beef Sirloin, Beef Blade Roast, Smoked Pork Shoulder Roll, Pork Shoulder Steaks, Ham with Bone in, Ground Meat, Fresh Fish and Seafood, Lamb, and Pork Chops	Poultry, Bulk Pork Sausage, Country-style Ribs, Beef Short Ribs, Lamb Shanks, Ham Shanks, and Oxtail

Smart Ways to Stretch Meat

Stretching meat economically takes talent. It means finding just the right combination of sauces, seasonings, biscuits, or pasta to go along with meat. One way to save money and make meat go further at the same time is to make your own homemade mixes.

Included in this section are a number of make-ahead mixes for sauces, gravies, stuffing cubes, noodles, pastry, lemon butter, and biscuits. These mixes can be substituted for their commercial equivalents. What's more, they are easy to make and convenient to keep on hand for emergency situations.

Accompanying these mixes are one or more recipes showing how to use them. But don't stop there. Experiment with your favorite recipes. You'll be surprised by the flavorful results.

Here are the ingredients for *Herb Stuffing Cubes*, upper left; *White Sauce Mix*, upper right; *Marinara Sauce*, lower right; and *Lemon Pepper Butter*, lower left (see index for recipe page numbers.)

Money-saving homemade mixes

Frozen Beef Starter

Prepare meat mixture ahead and freeze. Then, use it to prepare the recipes on this page—

    3 beaten eggs
    2 cups soft bread crumbs (3 slices)
    1 cup chopped celery
    1 cup chopped onion
    1 cup shredded carrot
    3 pounds ground beef

Combine first 5 ingredients and 1 teaspoon salt. Mix in beef. In large skillet cook half the mixture at a time till lightly browned and still moist. Stir to break up large pieces. Cool quickly. Seal in 2-cup portions in moisture-vaporproof containers. Label; freeze. Makes five 2-cup portions.

To thaw: In saucepan or skillet add ¼ cup water to 2 cups frozen meat mixture. Cook, covered, over low heat for 15 minutes; break up meat with a fork. Cover; cook 5 minutes longer. Substitute 2 cups Frozen Beef Starter for 1 pound browned ground beef.

Oriental Beef Sandwich

    2 cups Frozen Beef Starter
    ½ cup chopped onion
    1 clove garlic, minced
    1 tablespoon sugar
    1 teaspoon cornstarch
    ¼ teaspoon ground ginger
    2 tablespoons soy sauce
    6 hamburger buns, split and toasted
      Green pepper rings

In saucepan add ¼ cup water to Frozen Beef Starter; cover tightly. Place over low heat for 15 minutes; break up with fork. Cover; cook 5 minutes longer. Add onion and garlic; cook, uncovered, till onion is tender. Combine sugar, cornstarch, and ginger. Add soy sauce and ⅓ cup cold water. Stir into meat mixture. Cook and stir till thickened and bubbly. Serve on toasted hamburger buns. Trim with green pepper rings. Serves 6.

Beef and Cabbage Skillet

    2 cups Frozen Beef Starter
    1 small head cabbage, cut in 6 wedges
    1 cup White Sauce Mix (see recipe,
      page 19)
    1 cup cold water
    ½ teaspoon celery seed
    ¼ teaspoon paprika
    ¼ teaspoon dried thyme, crushed
      Dash pepper
    ½ cup shredded American cheese
      (2 ounces)

In saucepan add ¼ cup water to Frozen Beef Starter; cover tightly. Place over low heat for 15 minutes; break up meat with fork. Cover; cook 5 minutes longer. Meanwhile, in a 10-inch skillet cook cabbage wedges, covered, in small amount of salted water till tender, about 10 minutes. Drain the cabbage wedges thoroughly; place in 9x1½-inch round baking pan or 9x9x2-inch square baking pan.

Stir the White Sauce Mix into the beef. Slowly blend in 1 cup cold water, celery seed, paprika, thyme, and pepper. Cook and stir till mixture thickens and bubbles. Spoon over cabbage. Bake at 350° for 10 to 12 minutes. Top with cheese. Return to oven till cheese melts, 1 to 2 minutes longer. Serves 6.

Zesty Hamburger Skillet

    2 cups Frozen Beef Starter
    1 16-ounce can mixed vegetables
    1 8-ounce can tomato sauce
    ½ teaspoon dried basil, crushed
    1 cup Seasoned Rice Mix (see recipe,
      page 21)

In saucepan combine Frozen Beef Starter, undrained mixed vegetables, tomato sauce, and basil. Cook over low heat till the frozen meat is thawed and the mixture is bubbly, 20 to 25 minutes. Add Seasoned Rice Mix; stir in carefully. Remove from heat. Cover and let stand 5 minutes. Serves 4.

Marinara Sauce

Keep on hand for Spaghetti with Meat Sauce—

3 large onions, quartered
6 medium carrots, cut in chunks
3 cloves garlic, minced
⅓ cup cooking oil
6 28-ounce cans tomatoes
1 tablespoon sugar

Place onions in blender container; cover with water. Cover; blend till chopped. Drain; set onions aside. Repeat with carrots. In large kettle cook onions, carrots, and garlic in oil till tender. Place tomatoes in blender, one can at a time; blend till chopped. Add to vegetables. Stir in sugar, 1 teaspoon salt, and ⅛ teaspoon pepper. Boil gently, uncovered, till of desired consistency, 1¼ to 1½ hours, stirring near end of cooking time. Cool. Pass through food mill. Cover and refrigerate or freeze. Makes 12 cups.

Spaghetti with Meat Sauce

1 pound ground beef
1 cup chopped onion
1 clove garlic, minced
5 cups Marinara Sauce
1 6-ounce can tomato paste
¼ cup snipped parsley
1 teaspoon dried basil, crushed
¼ teaspoon dried thyme, crushed
1 bay leaf
Hot cooked spaghetti
Grated Parmesan cheese

ENTERTAINING SPECIAL

In Dutch oven cook meat, onion, and garlic till meat is browned. Drain off fat. Add Marinara Sauce, tomato paste, parsley, basil, thyme, bay leaf, and 1 cup water. Simmer, uncovered, till of desired consistency, 30 to 45 minutes, stirring occasionally. Remove bay leaf. Serve over hot cooked spaghetti. Pass Parmesan cheese. Makes 6 servings.

Prepare *Spaghetti with Meat Sauce* the next time you entertain. The superb Italian flavor comes from the seasoned tomato *Marinara Sauce.* Complete the meal with crisp breadsticks and red wine.

Herb Stuffing Cubes

Try this mix as the basis for stuffings and for casseroles such as Tuna Stuffing Casserole—

15 slices white bread, cut in ½-inch
   cubes
3 tablespoons cooking oil
2 tablespoons instant minced onion
2 tablespoons dried parsley flakes
1 teaspoon garlic salt
½ teaspoon ground sage
¼ teaspoon pepper

Spread bread cubes evenly in a large shallow baking pan. Toast cubes at 300° till golden, 40 to 45 minutes, stirring once. Remove from oven; cool slightly. Combine oil, onion, parsley flakes, garlic salt, sage, and ¼ teaspoon pepper. Add to bread cubes; toss lightly to coat. Store cubes in tightly covered containers till needed. Makes 6½ cups.

Tuna Stuffing Casserole

2 medium zucchini, sliced ½ inch thick
1 6½- or 7-ounce can tuna, drained
¾ cup shredded carrot
½ cup chopped onion
5 tablespoons margarine or butter
2¼ cups Herb Stuffing Cubes
1 10½-ounce can condensed cream of
   chicken soup
½ cup dairy sour cream

Halve zucchini slices. Cook in boiling salted water till tender; drain. Flake tuna. Cook carrot and onion in *4 tablespoons* margarine till tender. Add tuna, *1½ cups* Herb Stuffing Cubes, soup, and sour cream. Stir in zucchini. Turn into 2-quart casserole. Melt remaining margarine; toss with remaining cubes. Sprinkle over casserole. Bake at 350° for 30 to 40 minutes. Serves 6.

Tuna Stuffing Casserole is a perfect main course for an economical meal. This easy casserole combines sliced zucchini, carrot, onion, tuna, dairy sour cream, and homemade *Herb Stuffing Cubes.*

Lemon-Pepper Butter

An excellent topper for baked potatoes or recipes such as Lemon-Peppered Minute Steaks—

In mixing bowl cream 1 cup margarine or butter (½ pound) till light and fluffy. Add 2 tablespoons snipped chives, ¾ teaspoon grated lemon peel, 2 tablespoons lemon juice, and ¼ teaspoon freshly ground black pepper. Mix thoroughly, blending well. Store in tightly covered container in refrigerator till needed. Makes 2 cups.

Lemon-Peppered Minute Steaks

    4 beef cubed steaks
    ¼ teaspoon dry mustard
    ¼ cup Lemon-Pepper Butter
    1 2-ounce can mushroom stems and
        pieces, drained
    1 teaspoon Worcestershire sauce
    2 tablespoons Lemon-Pepper Butter
    1 cup Seasoned Rice Mix (see
        recipe, page 21), prepared

Sprinkle meat with mustard and ½ teaspoon salt. Melt the ¼ cup Lemon-Pepper Butter. Brown the steaks on both sides in butter; cook over high heat 1 minute more. Remove to warm platter. Add mushrooms, Worcestershire, and 3 tablespoons water to drippings. Bring to boiling. Return steaks to skillet; heat through. Add the 2 tablespoons Lemon-Pepper Butter to hot prepared Seasoned Rice Mix. Serve with steaks. Serves 4.

Homemade Noodles

Add your own special touch to any recipe that calls for noodles by making them yourself—

Combine 1 beaten egg, 2 tablespoons milk, and ½ teaspoon salt. Add enough all-purpose flour to make a stiff dough (about 1 cup). Roll dough very thin on a floured surface; let stand 20 minutes. Roll up loosely; slice ¼ inch wide. Unroll, spread out, and dry 2 hours. Store in container till needed.

To prepare noodles: Drop into boiling soup or boiling, salted water and cook, uncovered, about 10 minutes. Makes 3 cups.

Pastry Mix

If you need a piecrust, use this mix. It works especially well in Green Onion-Bacon Quiche—

Stir 6 cups all-purpose flour and 1 tablespoon salt together. Cut in 2 cups shortening till pieces resemble small peas. Store in tightly covered container in refrigerator till needed. Makes enough mix for three 2-crust pies or six 1-crust pastry shells.

For one 2-crust 8- or 9-inch pie or two 1-crust 8- or 9-inch pie shells, sprinkle 5 to 7 tablespoons cold water over 3 cups pastry mix, one tablespoon at a time. Toss with fork between tablespoon of water. Divide dough in half; form into 2 balls. Roll on floured surface till ⅛ inch thick.

To make 1-crust pastry shells: Fit pastry into pie plate. Trim pastry ½ to 1 inch beyond edge; fold under and flute. Prick bottom and sides well with fork. Bake at 450° till golden brown, 10 to 12 minutes.

To make 2-crust pies: Trim lower crust even with rim of pie plate. Cut slits in top crust. Lift pastry over well-filled pie. Trim ½ inch beyond edge. Tuck top crust under edge of lower crust. Flute edge. Bake as directed in the recipe.

Green Onion-Bacon Quiche

    6 slices bacon
    ¼ cup sliced green onion
        Pastry for 1-crust 8-inch pie
    1 cup shredded Swiss cheese
    3 beaten eggs
    1 cup milk
    ½ teaspoon dry mustard
        Dash ground nutmeg

Cook bacon till crisp; drain, reserving 1 tablespoon drippings. Crumble bacon. Cook onion in drippings till tender. Roll out pastry. Line 8-inch pie plate with pastry (do not prick); flute edges. Bake at 325° for 10 minutes. Layer cheese over bottom of pastry. Add bacon and onion. Combine eggs, milk, seasonings, and ¼ teaspoon salt. Pour over cheese. Bake at 325° till set, 45 to 48 minutes. Let stand 10 minutes before serving. Trim with parsley, if desired. Serves 6.

Seasoned Coating Mix

A versatile coating mixture for chicken, pork, or fish. Try it on the following two recipes —

2 cups fine dry bread crumbs
2 tablespoons onion powder
1 tablespoon salt
2 teaspoons poultry seasoning
½ teaspoon garlic powder
½ teaspoon paprika
½ teaspoon dried thyme, crushed
⅛ teaspoon cayenne

In bowl mix together bread crumbs, onion powder, salt, poultry seasoning, garlic powder, paprika, thyme, and cayenne. Store in tightly covered container till needed. Makes 2 ⅓ cups coating mix.

To use coating mix: Dip chicken pieces, pork chops, or fish fillets in milk, then in coating mix. Shake off excess coating mix. Bake or cook according to recipe directions.

Crispy Baked Chicken

1 2½- to 3-pound ready-to-cook broiler-fryer chicken, cut up
½ cup milk
¾ cup Seasoned Coating Mix

Brush chicken pieces with milk. Pat Seasoned Coating Mix onto each piece; shake off excess coating mix. Place chicken pieces, skin side up, in a lightly greased 15½x10½x1-inch baking pan. Bake at 375° till chicken is done, about 1 hour. Makes 4 servings.

Oven-Baked Pork Chops

6 pork rib chops, cut ¾ inch thick
• • •
⅓ cup milk
½ cup Seasoned Coating Mix

Trim excess fat from pork chops; discard. Dip chops in milk, then in Seasoned Coating Mix, covering both sides. Shake off excess coating mix. Place on rack in a 16½x11x2-inch roasting pan. Bake at 350° till pork chops are tender, about 50 minutes. Serves 6.

Beef Gravy Base

Use with roasts, potatoes, or in recipes —

1⅓ cups nonfat dry milk powder
¾ cup all-purpose flour
2 tablespoons instant beef bouillon granules
¾ teaspoon dried thyme, crushed
½ cup margarine or butter
• • •
Few drops Kitchen Bouquet

Combine dry milk powder, flour, bouillon granules, and thyme. Cut in margarine or butter till pieces resemble cornmeal. Store in a tightly covered container in the refrigerator till needed. Makes 2½ cups gravy base, enough for 5 cups gravy.

To make Beef Gravy: In saucepan slowly blend 1 cup cold water into ½ cup Beef Gravy Base. Cook and stir till mixture is thickened and bubbly; cook 1 minute more. Stir in Kitchen Bouquet. Makes 1 cup gravy.

Creamy Chicken Gravy Base

Handy to use when you need one or two cups of creamy gravy in a hurry. It also can be used as a base for all kinds of casseroles —

1⅓ cups nonfat dry milk powder
¾ cup all-purpose flour
2 tablespoons instant chicken bouillon granules
¾ teaspoon ground sage
½ cup margarine or butter
• • •
Few drops yellow food coloring (optional)

Combine dry milk powder, flour, chicken bouillon granules, and sage. Cut in margarine or butter till pieces resemble cornmeal. Store in a tightly covered container in the refrigerator till needed. Makes about 3 cups gravy base, enough for 6 cups gravy.

To make Chicken Gravy: In saucepan slowly blend 1 cup cold water into ½ cup Creamy Chicken Gravy Base. Cook and stir till mixture is thickened and bubbly. Cook 1 minute more. Add yellow food coloring, if desired. Makes 1 cup.

White Sauce Mix

Choose this mix anytime you need a white sauce and to prepare the following recipes—

1⅓ cups nonfat dry milk powder
¾ cup all-purpose flour
1½ teaspoons salt
¼ teaspoon white pepper
½ cup margarine or butter

In mixing bowl stir together nonfat dry milk powder, flour, salt, and pepper. Cut in margarine till pieces resemble cornmeal. Store in tightly covered container in refrigerator till needed. Makes 3 cups sauce mix.

Thin White Sauce: Slowly blend 1 cup cold water into ⅓ cup White Sauce Mix. Cook and stir over medium heat till thickened and bubbly. Cook 1 minute more. Makes 1 cup.

Medium White Sauce: Slowly blend 1 cup cold water into ⅔ cup White Sauce Mix. Cook and stir till thickened and bubbly. Cook 1 minute more. Makes about 1 cup.

Thick White Sauce: Slowly blend 1 cup cold water into 1 cup White Sauce Mix. Cook and stir over medium heat till thickened and bubbly. Cook 1 minute more. Makes 1¼ cups.

Salmon Newburg

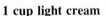

1 cup light cream
½ cup White Sauce Mix
3 beaten egg yolks
3 tablespoons dry white wine
2 teaspoons lemon juice
¼ teaspoon salt
¼ teaspoon dried tarragon, crushed
1 16-ounce can salmon, drained, bones and skin removed, and broken in chunks
Toast cups

Slowly blend cream and ½ cup cold water into White Sauce Mix. Cook and stir over low heat till thickened. Stir a moderate amount of hot mixture into egg yolks. Return egg yolk mixture to saucepan. Cook and stir over low heat till thickened and bubbly. Remove from heat; stir in wine, lemon juice, salt, and tarragon. Add salmon to mixture. Heat. Spoon into toast cups. Serves 4.

Cheesy Ham Casserole

1⅓ cups White Sauce Mix
½ cup shredded sharp American cheese (2 ounces)
1 teaspoon prepared mustard
2 beaten egg yolks
1½ cups elbow macaroni, cooked and drained (3 cups cooked)
1½ cups diced fully cooked ham
1 cup cream-style cottage cheese
⅓ cup finely chopped dill pickle
1½ cups soft bread crumbs
2 tablespoons margarine, melted

Slowly blend 2 cups cold water into White Sauce Mix. Cook and stir till thickened. Cook 1 minute more. Add shredded cheese and mustard; cook and stir till cheese melts. Stir a moderate amount of hot mixture into egg yolks; return to remaining hot mixture. Cook and stir till bubbly. Stir in macaroni, ham, cottage cheese, and pickle. Turn into 2-quart casserole. Combine crumbs and margarine; sprinkle atop casserole. Bake at 350° for 40 to 50 minutes. Serves 8.

Beef-Onion Casserole

2 medium onions, cut in wedges
1 pound ground beef
⅔ cup White Sauce Mix
1 teaspoon instant beef bouillon granules
1¼ cups cold water
2 cups Herb Stuffing Cubes (see recipe, page 16)
1 tablespoon margarine or butter, melted
½ cup shredded Swiss cheese (2 ounces)

In skillet cook onions and beef till meat is browned and onions are tender. Drain off fat. To skillet add White Sauce Mix, and bouillon granules. Blend water slowly into meat mixture. Cook and stir till thickened and bubbly. Stir in *1½ cups* of the Herb Stuffing Cubes. Turn into a 1½-quart casserole. Crush remaining stuffing cubes slightly; toss with margarine. Spoon atop casserole. Bake, uncovered, at 350° for 20 minutes. Sprinkle with cheese; bake till cheese melts, 2 to 3 minutes more. Makes 4 servings.

Tonight, surprise your hungry family by serving them *Corned Beef Stew*. They'll love its home-cooked flavor. Top this mixture of corned beef, split pea soup, and mixed vegetables with parsley dumplings.

Basic Biscuit Mix

Prepare the mix ahead and use when needed—

>   10 cups all-purpose flour
>   1¼ cups nonfat dry milk powder
>   ⅓ cup baking powder
>   4 teaspoons salt
>   1½ cups shortening that does not
>   require refrigeration

In large mixing bowl stir flour, dry milk powder, baking powder, and salt together thoroughly. Cut shortening into dry ingredients till mixture resembles coarse cornmeal.

Store mix in a tightly covered container up to six weeks at room temperature. For longer storage, place mix in freezer containers and freeze. Makes about 15 cups.

To measure: Spoon Basic Biscuit Mix lightly into measuring cup; level with spatula.

Corned Beef Stew

>   2 11¼-ounce cans condensed split pea
>   with ham soup
>   1 12-ounce can corned beef,
>   chilled and cubed
>   1 8½-ounce can mixed vegetables
>   1 cup Basic Biscuit Mix
>   1 beaten egg

In Dutch oven combine soup, beef, vegetables, and 2 cups water. Bring to boiling. Combine Basic Biscuit Mix, egg, and ⅓ cup water. Stir just till all ingredients are moistened. Drop batter from rounded tablespoons atop bubbling soup, making 4 to 6 dumplings. Sprinkle dumplings with dried parsley flakes, if desired. Cover tightly. Reduce heat; simmer 15 to 18 minutes (do not lift cover). Stir soup mixture before serving. Serves 4 to 6.

Basic Biscuits

3 cups Basic Biscuit Mix
¾ cup water

Turn Basic Biscuit Mix into a mixing bowl; make a well. Add the water all at once. Stir quickly with fork just till dough follows fork around bowl. On lightly floured surface knead dough 10 to 12 strokes. Roll or pat to ½-inch thickness. Dip 2½-inch biscuit cutter in flour; cut dough straight down. Bake the biscuits on ungreased baking sheet at 450° for 10 to 12 minutes. Makes 10 biscuits.

Beef and Cheese Biscuit Bake

1 pound ground beef
½ cup chopped onion
1 beaten egg
½ cup water
½ cup shredded Swiss cheese (2 ounces)
2 tablespoons snipped parsley
¼ teaspoon salt
   Dash bottled hot pepper sauce
2 teaspoons all-purpose flour
2 cups Basic Biscuit Mix
½ cup water
¼ cup grated Parmesan cheese
2 tablespoons salad dressing or mayonnaise
• • •
1 cup Beef Gravy (see recipe, page 18)

In skillet brown the ground beef and chopped onion; drain off the excess fat. Combine the beaten egg, ½ cup water, cheese, parsley, salt, and hot pepper sauce. Sprinkle flour over meat mixture and stir in. Add the egg mixture; cook, stirring constantly, till mixture is bubbly. Remove from heat.

Combine the Basic Biscuit Mix, the ½ cup water, Parmesan cheese, and salad dressing or mayonnaise. Pat half the biscuit mixture into a greased 8x8x2-inch baking pan. Spoon meat mixture over dough in pan. On lightly floured surface roll remaining dough to an 8x8-inch square; place over meat. Bake at 400° for 25 to 30 minutes. Serve hot with the Beef Gravy. Makes 6 servings.

Seasoned Rice Mix

Flavor main dishes with this meat stretcher—

6 cups uncooked packaged precooked rice
3 tablespoons dried parsley flakes
2 tablespoons instant beef *or* chicken bouillon granules
2 tablespoons instant minced onion

Combine the rice, parsley flakes, beef or chicken bouillon granules, and onion. Stir together thoroughly. Store in tightly closed container. Makes 6 cups mix.

For Seasoned Rice: Bring 1 cup water to boiling. Stir in 1 cup Seasoned Rice Mix; cover. Let stand 5 minutes. Makes 2 cups.

Chicken Liver-Rice Milanese

½ cup chopped celery
3 tablespoons margarine or butter
1 2-ounce can mushroom stems and pieces, drained
1 cup Seasoned Rice Mix
½ pound chicken livers, halved

In a saucepan cook celery in *1 tablespoon* of the margarine till celery is tender but not brown. Add mushrooms, Seasoned Rice Mix, and 1 cup water. Bring to boiling. Remove from heat; cover. Let stand 10 minutes. In a skillet heat chicken livers in remaining margarine till livers are cooked, about 5 minutes. Serve chicken livers atop rice. Serves 4.

Fish and Rice Skillet

Heat 4 cups water, 2 tablespoons lemon juice, and 1 teaspoon salt to boiling. Add 1 pound fresh or frozen fish fillets; simmer, covered, till fish flakes easily, 5 to 10 minutes. Drain fish, reserving 2 cups liquid. Flake fish. Cook 1 cup chopped celery and 1 clove garlic, minced, in 2 tablespoons margarine till tender. Stir in 2 cups Seasoned Rice Mix, 2 teaspoons curry powder, the reserved liquid, and fish. Heat to boiling. Remove from heat; let stand, covered, 5 minutes. Stir in ½ cup dairy sour cream; heat through but *do not boil*. Makes 6 servings.

Make Meat Go Further

Corner the meat market with the meat-saving ideas featured in this section. Save with recipes that show you how to combine meat with potatoes, rice, or pasta. Or use the new textured vegetable proteins. These soy-based products can save money because when they are added to ground meat they increase its volume by as much as half.

Besides these ideas, there are other ways to make meat go further. Make the most of roasts by using planned-overs wisely. Add variety along with economy to your meals by preparing liver, heart, kidney, or tongue. Choose from recipes made with frankfurters, pork sausage, or luncheon meat. Or eliminate leftover problems by selecting main dish salads, sandwiches, and soups or chowders that use leftover cooked meat.

Tempting recipes that will make your meat go further: *Enriched Meat Loaf* (see recipe, page 31); *Stuffed Baked Potatoes* (see recipe, page 66); and *Pork Marengo* (see recipe, page 50).

Make the most of beef

Consider boneless roasts when looking for beef bargains. Because they provide a greater number of servings per pound than cuts with bone, these meat cuts often save you money. Buy a piece of boneless beef and prepare it as a roast. Before serving, refrigerate or freeze the extra cooked meat to use in recipes such as Cheese-Topped Beef Bake, Oven Beef Hash, or Dipped Beef Sandwiches.

Braised Rolled Rump Roast

In Dutch oven brown a rolled beef rump roast on all sides in 2 tablespoons hot shortening. Sprinkle lightly with salt and pepper. Add about ½ cup water. Cover tightly and simmer till meat is fork-tender (about 2½ hours for a 4-pound roast). Plan on 6 servings per pound of meat as purchased.

Oven Beef Hash

    2 cups finely chopped cooked potato
    1 13-ounce can evaporated milk
        (1⅔ cups)
  1½ cups finely chopped cooked beef
  1¼ cups finely crushed rich round
        crackers (about 32 crackers)
    ½ cup shredded carrot
    ⅓ cup finely chopped onion
    ⅓ cup snipped parsley
    1 tablespoon Worcestershire sauce
    ¾ teaspoon salt
    ⅛ teaspoon pepper
    ⅛ teaspoon dried oregano, crushed
    1 tablespoon margarine or butter,
        melted

Lightly stir together potato, evaporated milk, beef, *1 cup* of the crushed crackers, carrot, onion, parsley, Worcestershire sauce, and seasonings. Turn into 1½-quart casserole. Combine remaining crumbs and melted margarine or butter; sprinkle atop casserole. Bake, covered, at 350° till heated through, 35 to 40 minutes. Makes 4 to 6 servings.

Dipped Beef Sandwiches

In a skillet combine one 10½-ounce can condensed beef broth, ⅔ cup water, 1 tablespoon snipped parsley, 1 small bay leaf, ¼ teaspoon onion powder, and ¼ teaspoon dry mustard. Add 12 thin slices cooked roast beef. Simmer, uncovered, 10 minutes. Remove bay leaf. Lift beef slices from broth and serve 3 slices on each of 4 split hard rolls. Serve broth in small bowls as a dip with each sandwich. Makes 4 sandwiches.

Cheese-Topped Beef Bake

    2 tablespoons chopped onion
    2 tablespoons cooking oil
    2 tablespoons all-purpose flour
    ¾ teaspoon salt
    ½ teaspoon sugar
    ¼ teaspoon dried basil, crushed
    ⅛ teaspoon pepper
    1 16-ounce can tomatoes, cut up
    1 16-ounce can cut green beans, drained
  1½ cups chopped cooked beef
    1 teaspoon instant beef bouillon
        granules
    ½ teaspoon Worcestershire sauce
    1 cup Basic Biscuit Mix (see recipe,
        page 20)
    ¼ teaspoon dry mustard
    2 tablespoons margarine or butter
    ½ cup milk
    ½ cup shredded sharp American cheese
        (2 ounces)

In a skillet cook onion in oil until tender. Stir in flour, salt, sugar, basil, and pepper. Add next 5 ingredients. Cover and simmer the mixture 10 minutes. Meanwhile, combine Basic Biscuit Mix and dry mustard. Cut in margarine; stir in milk till well blended. Stir in cheese. Roll dough out on floured surface to a rectangle ½ inch thick; cut into 6 wedges. Turn beef mixture into 10x6x1½-inch baking dish. Top with biscuit wedges. Bake at 400° about 20 minutes. Makes 6 servings.

Main Dish Peach-Beef Toss

4 cups torn romaine
3 cups torn spinach
1½ cups cooked beef cut in strips
3 medium peaches, peeled, pitted,
and sliced (1½ cups)
1 avocado, peeled, pitted, and sliced
12 cherry tomatoes, halved

• • •

Horseradish Dressing

Combine the romaine, spinach, beef strips, peaches, avocado, and cherry tomatoes in a salad bowl. Toss salad with Horseradish Dressing. Serve immediately. Serves 6.

Horseradish Dressing: In screw-top jar combine ½ cup salad oil, 3 tablespoons vinegar, 1 teaspoon prepared horseradish, ½ teaspoon Worcestershire sauce, ½ teaspoon salt, ⅛ teaspoon pepper, and 2 drops bottled hot pepper sauce. Cover; shake well.

Chef's Salad

1 cup dairy sour cream
1 3-ounce package cream cheese,
softened
⅓ cup milk
4 green onions, sliced
1 teaspoon prepared mustard
½ teaspoon paprika
¼ teaspoon salt
6½ cups torn lettuce
2 cups cooked roast beef, pork,
turkey, *or* ham cut in strips
1 cup cherry tomatoes, halved
4 ounces sharp American cheese,
cup in strips
3 hard-cooked eggs, sliced
1 medium cucumber, sliced

In a bowl combine sour cream, softened cream cheese, milk, green onions, prepared mustard, paprika, and salt; beat till smooth. Cover and chill while preparing salad.

In large salad bowl combine torn lettuce, meat, cherry tomatoes, cheese strips, hard-cooked egg slices, and cucumber; toss gently. Serve the salad with the chilled dressing. Makes 6 servings.

Beef-Macaroni Italiano

1 cup elbow macaroni
⅓ cup water
½ envelope onion soup mix (¼ cup)
1 16-ounce can tomatoes, cut up
2 tablespoons all-purpose flour
1 teaspoon salt
½ teaspoon dried oregano, crushed
Dash pepper
1½ cups cubed cooked beef

• • •

½ cup shredded Monterey Jack
cheese (2 ounces)
2 tablespoons grated Parmesan cheese

Cook the macaroni according to package directions. Drain and set aside. Combine the water and onion soup mix; let stand 5 minutes. In saucepan stir the undrained tomatoes into the flour. Add soup mixture, salt, oregano, and pepper. Cook and stir till thickened and bubbly. Stir in the beef and macaroni.

Turn into 1½-quart casserole. Bake at 350°, uncovered, for 20 minutes. Stir in shredded Monterey Jack cheese; sprinkle Parmesan on top. Bake 5 minutes more. Makes 4 servings.

Beef-Cabbage Soup

4 cups coarsely shredded cabbage
(1 small head)
1 28-ounce can tomatoes, cut up
2 cups cubed cooked beef, pork, *or*
lamb
1 10½-ounce can condensed beef broth
1 soup can water (1⅓ cups)
1 cup chopped onion
1 tart apple, peeled and diced
2 tablespoons lemon juice
1 tablespoon sugar
1 teaspoon salt
¼ teaspoon pepper

In Dutch oven or large kettle combine the shredded cabbage, undrained tomatoes, meat, condensed beef broth, water, onion, apple, lemon juice, sugar, salt, and pepper. Bring the mixture to boiling; reduce heat. Simmer, covered, till cabbage is tender, about 30 minutes. Ladle into soup bowls. Serves 8.

Top left: Make the most of beef by preparing *Braised Rolled Rump Roast* (see recipe, page 24). Before serving, refrigerate some of the meat to make casseroles and sandwiches.

Bottom Left: *Dipped Beef Sandwiches* (see recipe, page 24) are easy to fix. This satisfying sandwich features planned-over beef on a hard roll with plenty of gravy.

Top Right: *Main Dish Peach-Beef Toss* (see recipe, page 25) combines romaine, spinach, cooked beef, peaches, tomatoes, avocado, and *Horseradish Dressing* into an appetizing salad.

Bottom Right: Serve *Cheese-Topped Beef Bake* (see recipe, page 24) for a change of pace. This casserole consists of a beef, tomato, and green bean mixture topped with biscuits.

Beef and Cheese Wedges

  1 cup Basic Biscuit Mix (see recipe,
     page 20)
  1 beaten egg yolk
  2 tablespoons milk
1½ pounds ground beef
  ½ cup chopped onion
  1 clove garlic, minced
  ½ teaspoon Italian seasoning
  1 beaten egg
  1 beaten egg white
  2 cups cream-style cottage cheese
  ½ cup shredded Swiss cheese

Stir Basic Biscuit Mix, egg yolk, and milk together. Form into a ball. Roll dough ⅛ inch thick on floured surface; fit into 9-inch pie plate and flute edge. In skillet combine ground beef, onion, garlic, Italian seasoning, ½ teaspoon salt, and ¼ teaspoon pepper. Cook till beef is browned. Drain off excess fat. Spoon meat mixture into biscuit shell. Combine egg, egg white, and cottage cheese; spoon over meat mixture. Bake at 375° for 15 minutes. Top with the shredded Swiss cheese; bake 10 minutes more. Serves 8.

Lasagne Americana

Cook 8 lasagne noodles. Melt 2 tablespoons margarine; stir in 2 tablespoons all-purpose flour, ¼ teaspoon salt, and dash pepper. Add 1½ cups chicken broth; cook and stir till thickened. Combine 2 beaten egg yolks and 1 cup milk. Stir in a moderate amount of hot broth mixture; return to hot mixture. Cook over low heat till slightly thickened. Cook 1 pound ground beef and ½ cup chopped onion till meat is brown; drain fat. Stir in one 6-ounce can chopped mushrooms, drained; *1 cup* of the sauce; 1 teaspoon salt; and dash pepper. Simmer 2 to 3 minutes.

Combine one 10-ounce package frozen chopped spinach, ¼ cup chicken broth, 1 tablespoon lemon juice, and ¼ teaspoon salt; cook 5 minutes and drain. Spoon *half* the meat into 12x7½x2-inch baking dish; top with *half* the sauce, *4* noodles, and spinach. Repeat layers. Cover; bake at 350° for 35 to 40 minutes. Serves 6.

Beef-Broccoli Pie

  1 pound ground beef
  ¼ cup chopped onion
  2 tablespoons all-purpose flour
  ¾ teaspoon salt
  ¼ teaspoon garlic salt
1¼ cups milk
  1 3-ounce package cream cheese,
     softened
  1 beaten egg
  1 10-ounce package frozen chopped
     broccoli, cooked and
     well drained
       • • •
     Pastry for 2-crust 9-inch pie
     (see recipe, page 15)
  4 ounces Monterey Jack cheese
     Milk

In a medium skillet brown the beef and onion; drain off fat. Stir in the flour, salt, and garlic salt. Add the 1¼ cups milk and softened cream cheese; cook and stir till mixture is smooth and bubbly. Add a moderate amount of the hot creamed mixture to the beaten egg; return to the mixture in the skillet. Cook and stir over medium heat till the mixture is thickened, 1 to 2 minutes. Stir in cooked chopped broccoli. Set aside. Line a 9-inch pie plate with *half* the pastry. Spoon the hot meat mixture into the pastry shell. Cut the Monterey Jack cheese into slices. Arrange the cheese slices atop the meat mixture. Adjust the top crust of the meat pie. Seal. Use a fork to make perforations in the piecrust in spoke-fashion or slash for escape of steam.

Brush the top of the beef pie with a little milk. Bake at 350° for 40 to 45 minutes. If the pastry browns too quickly, cover edge of the crust with foil during the last 20 minutes. Let the pie stand 10 minutes before serving. Makes 6 servings.

Full of flavor

Beef-Broccoli Pie has a golden crust made →
from *Pastry Mix* (see recipe, page 17). Between the top and bottom crusts, Monterey Jack and cream cheese moisten the rich filling.

Cheeseburger Loaf

1 beaten egg
1 10¾-ounce can condensed Cheddar
    cheese soup
½ cup soft bread crumbs
½ cup chopped dill pickle
¼ cup chopped onion
¼ teaspoon salt
⅛ teaspoon pepper
1½ pounds ground beef

Combine egg, ⅓ *cup* of the cheese soup, crumbs, pickle, onion, salt, and pepper. Add ground beef; mix well. Shape into loaf. Place in shallow baking pan. Bake at 350° for 1¼ hours. Place on platter. Heat remaining soup; pour over loaf to serve. Serves 6.

Meat Loaf Potato Roll-Up

All this and only 289 calories per serving—

Combine 2 beaten eggs, ⅓ cup tomato sauce, ½ cup finely crushed saltine crackers, ¼ cup finely chopped onion, 2 tablespoons chopped green pepper, and ¾ teaspoon salt. Add 1½ pounds lean ground beef; mix well. Pat to a 10x8-inch rectangle; set aside. Prepare packaged instant mashed potatoes (enough for 3 servings), following package directions, *except omit butter.* Mix in 1 tablespoon snipped parsley and ⅛ teaspoon *each* dried thyme, crushed, and dried marjoram, crushed. Spoon mixture in center of meat. Fold sides over potato; seal. Place, seam side down, on 15½x10½x1-inch baking pan. Bake at 350° for 45 minutes. Serves 8.

Meat Loaf Potato Roll-Up is an economical mainstay that will delight your family and guests alike. Mashed potatoes, thyme, marjoram, and parsley combine to produce the flavorful filling.

Stroganoff Loaf

1 beaten egg
⅔ cup milk
¾ cup quick-cooking rolled oats
1 teaspoon salt
1 teaspoon Worcestershire sauce
¼ teaspoon pepper
1½ pounds ground beef
1 3-ounce can chopped mushrooms, drained
½ cup chopped onion
2 tablespoons margarine or butter
½ cup dairy sour cream

Combine first 6 ingredients; add beef and mix well. Place half the meat in an 8½x4½x2½-inch loaf pan; make a well in center. Brown the mushrooms and onion in margarine or butter. Stir in sour cream and ¼ teaspoon salt; spoon into well. Top with remaining meat; seal. Bake at 350° for 1 hour. Let stand 5 minutes before removing from pan. Serves 6.

Pineapple Meat Loaf

1 15¼-ounce can crushed pineapple (juice pack)
2 beaten eggs
1 cup soft bread crumbs
2 tablespoons finely chopped onion
2 tablespoons soy sauce
½ teaspoon salt
1½ pounds ground beef
2 teaspoons cornstarch
2 teaspoons prepared mustard
¼ cup catsup
Few drops bottled hot pepper sauce

Drain crushed pineapple well, adding water to juice if necessary to equal 1 cup. Reserve juice for sauce. In mixing bowl combine eggs, bread crumbs, crushed pineapple, onion, soy, salt, and dash pepper. Add beef; mix well. Shape into a loaf. Place in 11x7½x1½-inch baking pan. Bake at 350° for 1¼ hours.

Meanwhile, in small saucepan blend together cornstarch and mustard. Stir in catsup, reserved pineapple juice, and hot pepper sauce. Cook and stir till thickened and bubbly. Pass with meat loaf. Makes 8 servings.

Surprise Meat Loaves

2 beaten eggs
¼ cup milk
1 slice rye bread, toasted and crumbled
2 tablespoons snipped parsley
1 tablespoon Worcestershire sauce
2 pounds ground beef
1 cup cubed Swiss cheese
1 cup chopped canned luncheon meat
1 tablespoon snipped parsley

Combine eggs, milk, crumbs, 2 tablespoons parsley, Worcestershire, ½ teaspoon salt, and dash pepper. Add beef; mix. Combine cheese, luncheon meat, and 1 tablespoon parsley. Divide beef mixture into 6 portions. Form each into an oval loaf around ⅓ cup of the cheese mixture. Place in 13x9x2-inch baking pan. Bake at 350° for 45 minutes. Serves 6.

Little Cranberry Loaves

Combine 1 beaten egg, 1 cup cooked rice, ½ cup tomato juice, ¼ cup chopped onion, and 1½ teaspoons salt. Mix in 1 pound ground beef. Shape into 5 loaves. Place in shallow baking pan. Combine one 16-ounce can whole cranberry sauce, ⅓ cup packed brown sugar, and 1 tablespoon lemon juice; spoon over loaves. Bake at 350° for 40 minutes. Serves 5.

Enriched Meat Loaf

This tasty meat loaf is shown on page 22 —

1 beef bouillon cube
½ cup boiling water
1 beaten egg
1 8-ounce can stewed tomatoes
½ cup wheat germ
½ cup nonfat dry milk powder
⅓ cup finely chopped onion
¼ cup soy grits
1 pound ground beef

Dissolve bouillon cube in water. Combine with next 6 ingredients and ¾ teaspoon salt. Add beef; mix well. Turn into a greased 8½x4½x2½-inch loaf pan. Bake at 350° for 1 hour. Makes 6 servings.

Best-Ever Chili

2 pounds ground beef
1 cup chopped onion
1 cup chopped green pepper
1 cup sliced celery
2 15½-ounce cans red kidney beans
2 16-ounce cans tomatoes, cut up
1 6-ounce can tomato paste
2 cloves garlic, minced
1 to 1½ tablespoons chili powder
2 teaspoons salt

In Dutch oven cook beef, onion, green pepper, and celery till meat is brown and vegetables are tender. Drain kidney beans, reserving liquid. Add beans and remaining ingredients. Cover; simmer 1 to 1½ hours. If desired, stir in some reserved bean liquid to make desired consistency. Serves 10.

Beefburger Stack-Ups

2 beaten eggs
¼ cup milk
1 teaspoon salt
1 teaspoon Worcestershire sauce
    Dash pepper
1½ pounds ground beef
    Packaged instant mashed potatoes
        (enough for 4 servings)
1 cup boiling water
½ cup dairy sour cream
¼ cup chopped green onion
2 tablespoons chopped canned pimiento
¼ teaspoon salt
3 slices sharp American cheese,
        cut in half
    Catsup, heated

Combine eggs, milk, 1 teaspoon salt, Worcestershire sauce, and pepper. Add beef and mix well. Form into 12 patties. Place one patty in *each* of 6 individual casserole dishes. Stir mashed potatoes into boiling water. Add sour cream, green onion, pimiento, and ¼ teaspoon salt; spoon over meat patties. Cover with remaining patties. Bake at 375° for 45 minutes. Top with cheese slice halves. Bake till cheese melts, about 2 minutes more. Serve with warm catsup. Makes 6 servings.

Calico Salisbury Steaks

These tempting steaks are shown on page 2 –

½ cup cooked rice
¼ cup chopped green pepper
¼ cup chopped onion
1 tablespoon snipped parsley
1 teaspoon salt
¼ teaspoon garlic salt
1½ pounds ground beef
    Salisbury Sauce

Combine rice, green pepper, onion, parsley, salt, garlic salt, and dash pepper. Add ground beef and mix well. Shape the mixture into four oval patties, 1 inch thick. Grill over hot coals for 15 minutes, turning once. Serve with Salisbury Sauce. If desired, thread pickle chunks and green olives on skewers; garnish each burger with kabob. Serves 4.

Salisbury Sauce: In medium saucepan thoroughly combine ¼ cup catsup; 2 tablespoons chili sauce; 1 teaspoon Worcestershire sauce; ½ teaspoon Kitchen Bouquet; and ¼ teaspoon dried basil, crushed. Stir in ⅔ cup water. Simmer, covered, for 15 minutes.

Beefy Garbanzo Casserole

1 pound ground beef
1 cup chopped onion
2 cloves garlic, minced
2 15-ounce cans garbanzo beans,
    drained
1 15-ounce can tomato sauce
½ cup water
1 teaspoon dried oregano, crushed
½ teaspoon salt
½ teaspoon ground cumin
¼ teaspoon pepper
2 bay leaves

In saucepan cook ground beef, onion, and garlic till meat is brown and onion is tender. Drain off fat. Stir in garbanzo beans, tomato sauce, water, oregano, salt, cumin, pepper, and bay leaves. Heat to boiling. Turn into 1½-quart casserole. Bake, covered, at 350° for 45 minutes. Remove bay leaves; stir before serving. Garnish with fresh onion rings, if desired. Makes 5 or 6 servings.

No-Crust Pizzas

    1 beaten egg
    1 8-ounce can pizza sauce
    ¼ cup fine dry bread crumbs
    ¼ cup finely chopped onion
    1 medium clove garlic, minced
1½ pounds ground beef
    1 cup shredded mozzarella cheese

Combine egg, ¼ *cup* of the pizza sauce, crumbs, onion, garlic, and ¾ teaspoon salt. Add meat; mix well. Divide in eight portions. On foil-lined shallow baking pan shape each portion to 3-inch circle, building up ¾-inch rim. Spoon remaining sauce on each pizza. Bake at 450° for 10 minutes. Sprinkle with cheese; bake 5 minutes more. Serves 8.

Fruited Corned Beef Squares

Combine 2 cups corn bread stuffing mix and ½ cup water. Add 1 beaten egg, two 15-ounce cans corned beef hash, 1 tablespoon chopped green pepper, and 1 teaspoon instant minced onion; mix well. Pat into an 8x8x2-inch baking pan. Bake at 350° for 20 minutes. Combine one 8¼-ounce can crushed pineapple, undrained; ¼ cup packed brown sugar; and 1 teaspoon soy sauce. Spoon over meat loaf. Bake 25 minutes more. Serves 8 or 9.

Jiffy Hash Patties

    ¼ cup chopped onion
    1 tablespoon margarine or butter
    1 8-ounce can tomato sauce
    ¼ cup chopped green pepper
    1 tablespoon sugar
    1 tablespoon Worcestershire sauce
    1 15-ounce can corned beef hash,
       chilled

Cook onion in margarine till tender but not brown. Add tomato sauce, green pepper, sugar, and Worcestershire; heat through. Open both ends of corned beef hash can and push hash out. Cut into 4 slices. Broil 2 inches from heat for 8 to 10 minutes. Do not turn. Serve with sauce. Serves 4.

Bean and Bacon Roast

Combine 2 tablespoons all-purpose flour, ½ teaspoon salt, ¼ teaspoon paprika, and dash pepper. Coat one 2-pound boneless beef rump roast with the flour mixture. In Dutch oven brown the roast on all sides in 2 tablespoons hot cooking oil. Remove from heat.

    In a bowl combine one 11½-ounce can condensed bean with bacon soup, ½ cup water, 1 teaspoon Kitchen Bouquet, and 1 bay leaf. Pour the mixture over the roast. Cover and simmer for 1 hour and 45 minutes, stirring the mixture occasionally.

    Add 4 to 6 carrots, halved; 8 to 12 small onions; and 1 medium green pepper, cut in pieces. Cover and simmer till the meat and vegetables are tender, about 45 minutes more. Discard the bay leaf; arrange the rump roast and the vegetables on a warm serving platter. Pass the soup mixture with roast for gravy. Makes 6 servings.

Check meat label

An alert shopper should read all the information on the supermarket meat labels. Besides the all-important cost of the package, look for the name of the meat cut, the government grade, the price per pound, and the weight. Note, too, whether the weight is stated in the decimals 2.50 or in pounds and ounces 2 lbs., 8 oz.

TRIPLE A
Food Market

Weight Lbs. Net.	THIS PKG.	Price Per Lb.
2.50	**$2.73**	1.09

BEEF ROAST
USDA CHOICE

Pineapple Pot Roast

    1 8¼-ounce can pineapple slices
    ¼ cup soy sauce
    3 tablespoons lemon juice
    2 tablespoons packed brown sugar
    ½ teaspoon dried basil, crushed
    1 clove garlic, minced
    1 4-pound beef blade pot roast
            • • •
    2 tablespoons cooking oil
    3 tablespoons cornstarch

Drain pineapple, reserving syrup; set aside slices. Add enough water to syrup to make 1½ cups. Combine syrup with next 5 ingredients. Place roast in shallow pan; pour soy mixture over. Cover; marinate at room temperature for 2 hours, turning meat occasionally. Drain, reserving marinade. In Dutch oven brown the meat in hot oil. Add *1 cup* reserved marinade. Cover and roast at 350° till tender, 2½ to 3 hours, basting often. During last 10 minutes, top with pineapple slices.

Remove meat to platter. Add reserved marinade and enough water to pan drippings to make 2 cups liquid. Stir ¼ cup cold water into cornstarch; stir into drippings. Cook and stir till thickened. Drizzle meat with some sauce; pass remaining. Serves 8.

Savory Blade Pot Roast

    1 3-pound beef blade pot roast
    2 tablespoons cooking oil
    ¼ cup wine vinegar
    ¼ cup cooking oil
    ¼ cup catsup
    2 tablespoons soy sauce
    2 tablespoons Worcestershire sauce
    1 teaspoon dried rosemary, crushed
    ½ teaspoon garlic powder
    ½ teaspoon dry mustard

In skillet brown the meat slowly in 2 tablespoons cooking oil. Sprinkle meat with salt. Combine remaining ingredients; pour over meat. Cover tightly and simmer till meat is tender, about 2 hours. Remove meat to warm platter. Skim excess fat from sauce; spoon sauce over meat. Makes 6 to 8 servings.

Herbed Steak Broil

    ½ cup clear French salad dressing
        with herbs and spices
    ½ cup dry sherry
    2 tablespoons sliced green onion
    1 tablespoon Worcestershire sauce
        Dash pepper
            • • •
    1 2½- to 3-pound beef chuck steak, cut
        1½ inches thick

Combine dressing, sherry, onion, Worcestershire, and pepper. Pour over meat in shallow dish. Marinate, covered, at room temperature several hours or refrigerate overnight, turning at least once and spooning sauce over occasionally. Drain, reserving marinade. Broil meat over hot coals for 40 to 50 minutes, turning every 10 to 15 minutes and brushing with marinade. Meat will be rare; cook longer for desired doneness. Serves 6 to 8.

Home-Style Flank Steak

    1 1½-pound beef flank steak
    2 tablespoons all-purpose flour
    2 tablespoons cooking oil
    1 cup water
    2 tablespoons snipped parsley
    1 teaspoon sugar
    1 teaspoon instant beef
        bouillon granules
    ½ teaspoon dried thyme, crushed
    ½ cup cold water
    3 tablespoons all-purpose flour

Score flank steak on one side; coat both sides with the 2 tablespoons flour. In medium skillet brown the meat on all sides in hot cooking oil. Season steak with salt and pepper. Add the 1 cup water, parsley, sugar, beef bouillon granules; and thyme. Cover and simmer till beef is tender, 1½ to 2 hours. Remove beef to warm platter. Measure pan juices; add enough water to make 1¼ cups. Stir the ½ cup water into the 3 tablespoons flour. Stir in pan juices. Cook, stirring constantly, till mixture thickens and bubbles. Pour part of the gravy over meat; pass remaining gravy. Makes 5 or 6 servings.

Pineapple, soy sauce, lemon juice, and brown sugar enhance the flavor of *Pineapple Pot Roast.* Serve this hearty headliner to satisfy family appetites and still keep the meat budget in line.

Vegetable-Stuffed Steaks

This attractive dish appears on the cover—

> 6 beef cubed steaks (about 1½ pounds total)
> ¾ cup French salad dressing
> 1½ cups shredded carrot
> ¾ cup finely chopped onion
> ¾ cup finely chopped green pepper
> ¾ cup finely chopped celery
> 6 slices bacon

Sprinkle steaks with 1 teaspoon salt and ¼ teaspoon pepper. Marinate, covered, in dressing for 30 to 60 minutes at room temperature. Simmer vegetables in ¼ cup water, covered, till crisp-tender, 7 to 8 minutes; drain well. Drain steaks; place about ⅓ cup vegetable mixture on each steak. Roll up jelly-roll fashion. Cut bacon slices in half crosswise. Wrap two half-pieces around each roll-up; secure with wooden picks. Broil steak rolls 3 to 4 inches from heat for 20 to 25 minutes, turning steaks occasionally. Serves 6.

Deviled Steak Strips

> 1½ pounds beef round steak
> ⅓ cup all-purpose flour
> ¼ cup chopped onion
> 1 clove garlic, minced
> ¼ cup margarine or butter
> ½ cup tomato sauce
> 2 tablespoons vinegar
> 2 teaspoons prepared horseradish
> 2 teaspoons prepared mustard
> Homemade Noodles (see recipe, page 17) or packaged noodles, cooked

Trim excess fat from meat. Cut meat into thin strips about 3 inches long; coat with flour. In skillet cook meat, onion, and garlic in margarine till meat is browned and onion is tender. Stir in tomato sauce, vinegar, horseradish, mustard, 2 cups water, ¾ teaspoon salt, and ¼ teaspoon pepper. Cover and simmer till meat is tender, about 45 minutes, stirring occasionally. Serve steak strips over hot cooked noodles. Makes 8 servings.

Textured vegetable proteins

Extend ground meat with textured vegetable proteins. Made from soybeans, they stretch the protein value and volume of ground meat while still keeping the meat's flavor.

Textured vegetable proteins are marketed in two ways—already combined with ground beef or in a granular form ready to blend with meat. The packaged supermarket mixture, which is labeled, usually contains 75 percent ground beef and 25 percent soy protein. For the homemade mixture, use a pound of ground beef and add the soy protein with the amount of liquid specified in label directions to yield about 1½ pounds.

Saucy Beef Meatballs

1 beaten egg
2 tablespoons milk
1 cup soft bread crumbs
½ teaspoon salt
1½ pounds ground beef-textured vegetable protein mixture
2 tablespoons all-purpose flour
2 tablespoons cooking oil
1 15-ounce can tomato sauce
1 3-ounce can chopped mushrooms
¼ cup dry white wine
1 tablespoon snipped parsley
½ teaspoon dried oregano, crushed
  Homemade Noodles (see recipe, page 17), cooked
  Grated Parmesan cheese

Combine beaten egg, milk, bread crumbs, salt, and dash pepper. Add ground beef-textured vegetable protein mixture; mix well. Shape into 24 meatballs. Coat lightly with flour. Brown the meatballs in hot oil in skillet. Drain off fat. Combine tomato sauce, undrained mushrooms, wine, parsley, and oregano; pour over meat. Cover; simmer 20 to 25 minutes. Serve over hot cooked noodles; sprinkle with Parmesan cheese. Makes 8 servings.

Family Skillet Supper

2 beaten eggs
½ cup water
½ cup chopped onion
¼ cup fine dry bread crumbs
2 tablespoons snipped parsley
1 teaspoon salt
¼ teaspoon pepper
1½ pounds ground beef-textured vegetable protein mixture
2 tablespoons margarine or butter, melted
6 large carrots, cut in pieces
8 small new potatoes, peeled
1 16-ounce can tomatoes
1 9-ounce package frozen cut green beans
  Gravy

Combine eggs, ½ cup water, onion, crumbs, parsley, salt, and pepper. Add ground beef-textured vegetable protein mixture; mix well. Shape into 2 loaves. In 12-inch skillet brown the meat loaves in margarine. Spoon off fat. Add next 4 ingredients. Sprinkle with salt and pepper to taste. Cover; cook 45 minutes. Remove meat loaves and vegetables to platter; keep warm. Serve with Gravy. Serves 8.

Gravy: Measure pan juices. Add enough water to make 1 cup. Return to skillet. Blend ¼ cup cold water into 2 tablespoons all-purpose flour. Stir into pan juices. Cook and stir till thickened and bubbly. Makes 1¼ cups.

One-Pan Spaghetti Dinner

1½ pounds ground beef-textured vegetable protein mixture
6 cups water
2 envelopes spaghetti sauce mix
1 6-ounce can tomato paste
1 teaspoon salt
8 ounces spaghetti, broken

In large saucepan brown the ground beef-textured vegetable protein mixture. Add water, spaghetti sauce mix, tomato paste, and salt; bring to boiling. Add uncooked spaghetti. Cover; cook, stirring often, till spaghetti is tender, 20 minutes. Serves 8.

Hamburger Omelets Foo Yong

    6 egg yolks
    ¾ pound ground beef-textured vegetable
        protein mixture
    1 5-ounce can bamboo shoots, drained
    ⅓ cup finely chopped onion
    2 tablespoons snipped parsley
    1 teaspoon salt
    ¼ teaspoon pepper
    6 stiffly beaten egg whites
    2 tablespoons margarine or butter
      Chinese Brown Sauce

Beat egg yolks till thick and lemon-colored. Blend in next 6 ingredients. Fold in egg whites. In large skillet melt margarine or butter. Using ⅓ cup mixture for each omelet, cook over medium heat 3 minutes on each side. Add more margarine, if needed. Serve with Chinese Brown Sauce. Makes 6 servings.

Chinese Brown Sauce: Melt 1 tablespoon margarine or butter. Blend in 2 teaspoons cornstarch and 1 teaspoon sugar. Add ½ cup water and 1½ tablespoons soy sauce. Cook and stir till mixture thickens. Makes ½ cup.

Applesauce-Beef Loaf

    1 beaten egg
    1 cup soft bread crumbs
    1 8½-ounce can applesauce
    2 tablespoons finely chopped onion
    2 teaspoons prepared mustard
    1 teaspoon dried celery flakes
    1½ pounds ground beef-textured vegetable
        protein mixture
    1 tablespoon packed brown sugar
    1 tablespoon vinegar
    ¼ teaspoon ground allspice

Combine egg, crumbs, ½ *cup* of the applesauce, onion, *1 teaspoon* mustard, celery flakes, ½ teaspoon salt, and dash pepper. Add ground beef-textured vegetable protein mixture and mix well. Shape into a round loaf. Place into a shallow baking pan. Make a depression in top of loaf. Combine remaining applesauce and mustard, sugar, vinegar, and allspice; pour into depression. Bake at 350° for 50 to 60 minutes. Serves 6 to 8.

Oriental Beef Ring

    1 3-ounce can chow mein noodles
    1 8-ounce can tomato sauce with onions
    2 beaten eggs
    ¼ cup finely chopped celery
    2 tablespoons soy sauce
    ¼ teaspoon ground ginger
    1½ pounds ground beef-textured vegetable
        protein mixture
    1 tablespoon packed brown sugar
    1 teaspoon soy sauce
    1 10-ounce package frozen peas
    1 tablespoon margarine or butter

Crush *1½ cups* of the noodles. Combine with ¾ *cup* of the tomato sauce; let stand 5 minutes. Combine next 4 ingredients and noodle mixture. Add ground beef-textured vegetable protein mixture; mix well. Press into greased 5-cup ring mold. Invert on foil-lined shallow baking pan; remove mold. Bake at 350° for 40 to 45 minutes. Combine remaining tomato sauce, sugar, and the 1 teaspoon soy sauce; brush on ring. Return to oven for 2 to 3 minutes. Meanwhile, cook peas according to package directions; drain. Toss with margarine; stir in remaining noodles. Serve peas in the center of meat ring. Serves 8.

Salad Burger Stack-Ups

    1 cup chopped onion
    1 cup chopped tomato
    ½ cucumber, thinly sliced
    ¼ cup chopped sweet pickle
    ¼ cup vinegar
    ¼ cup water
    2 tablespoons sugar
    1 teaspoon salt
    ⅛ teaspoon pepper
    1½ pounds ground beef-textured vegetable
        protein mixture

Combine the first 9 ingredients. Cover and chill mixture 2 hours; drain well. Mix ground beef-textured vegetable protein mixture, ½ teaspoon salt, and ⅛ teaspoon pepper. Shape into 8 patties. Grill over medium coals, turning once. Spoon vegetable mixture atop each burger. Season to taste. Serves 8.

Make the most of ham

Plan money-saving meals using the shank portion of a fully cooked ham. Although it has more bone than the butt portion, it is often attractively priced. Bake it to serve hot first. Then, remove the meat from the bone and refrigerate or wrap and freeze up to two months. You'll have planned-over ham to use in recipes such as Glazed Ham Patties.

Baked Ham Shank

Place one 5- to 7-pound fully cooked, smoked ham portion, fat side up, on rack in shallow roasting pan. Do not add water or a cover. Score the ham in diamonds (cut only ¼ inch deep), if desired. Insert a meat thermometer into the center of the thickest part of the meat, being sure that the thermometer tip does not touch any bone or fat. Heat the ham at 325° till meat thermometer registers 135° to 140°, 1¾ to 2¼ hours. Plan on 3 or 4 servings per pound of meat as purchased.

Glazed Ham Patties

   ½ cup finely chopped celery
   ¼ cup finely chopped onion
   2 tablespoons margarine or butter
2¼ cups soft bread crumbs
   ½ cup milk
   ½ teaspoon dry mustard
   ½ teaspoon curry powder
   1 beaten egg
   2 cups ground fully cooked ham
   2 tablespoons cooking oil
   ¼ cup apple jelly

Cook celery and onion in margarine till tender but not brown. Add crumbs, milk, dry mustard, and curry. Cook and stir 1 minute. Remove the mixture from heat; blend in egg. Stir in ham. Shape the mixture into 6 patties.

   Brown the patties in hot oil about 3 minutes on each side. Combine jelly and 1 tablespoon water; heat till jelly is melted. Serve the glaze over the patties. Serves 6.

Cauliflower-Ham Chowder

Serve everyone a generous portion —

   2 cups sliced cauliflower
   1 13¾-ounce can chicken broth
      (1¾ cups)
   1 cup milk *or* light cream
   1 10½-ounce can condensed cream of
      potato soup
   ¼ cup cold water
   2 tablespoons cornstarch
   ⅛ teaspoon white pepper
   2 cups diced fully cooked ham
   Thinly sliced green onion

In large saucepan cook the cauliflower, covered, in the chicken broth till almost tender, about 10 minutes. Do not drain the cauliflower. Set aside. In bowl gradually add the milk to the cream of potato soup; mix thoroughly. Slowly blend the water into cornstarch and white pepper; stir into the potato soup mixture. Pour the mixture over the cooked cauliflower; cook and stir the chowder till thickened and bubbly.

   Stir in the diced ham; simmer the chowder over low heat till heated through, about 10 minutes. Garnish the chowder with green onion. Makes 5 or 6 servings.

Curry-Ham-Rice Salad

   ½ cup salad dressing or mayonnaise
   2 teaspoons vinegar
   1 teaspoon curry powder
   1 cup Seasoned Rice Mix, prepared
      (see recipe, page 21)
   1 cup cubed fully cooked ham
   1 medium apple, chopped
   4 lettuce cups

In mixing bowl thoroughly combine the salad dressing or mayonnaise, vinegar, and curry powder. Add the prepared Seasoned Rice Mix, cubed ham, and the chopped apple. Chill the salad in the refrigerator. Serve the salad in lettuce cups. Makes 4 servings.

Vegetable-Ham Medley

1 beaten egg
1 17-ounce can cream-style corn
1 16-ounce can mixed vegetables,
    drained
1½ cups soft rye bread crumbs
2 teaspoons instant minced onion
1 teaspoon dry mustard
¼ teaspoon salt
¼ teaspoon dried marjoram, crushed
    Dash pepper
2 cups chopped fully cooked ham
1 4-ounce can mushroom stems and
    pieces, drained

• • •

1 tablespoon margarine or butter,
    melted

Combine beaten egg, cream-style corn, mixed vegetables, *1 cup* of the bread crumbs, instant minced onion, mustard, salt, marjoram, and pepper. Carefully stir in ham and mushrooms. Turn into a 1½-quart casserole. Combine the remaining ½ cup rye bread crumbs and margarine; sprinkle over top of casserole. Bake, uncovered, at 350° till heated through, 45 to 50 minutes. Makes 6 servings.

Denver Scramble

Quick and easy for late-night entertaining—

1 cup finely chopped fully
    cooked ham
1 2-ounce can mushroom stems
    and pieces, drained
¼ cup chopped onion
2 tablespoons chopped green pepper
2 tablespoons margarine or butter,
    melted
8 beaten eggs
⅓ cup milk

(ENTERTAINING SPECIAL)

In skillet cook ham, mushrooms, onion, and green pepper in margarine or butter till vegetables are tender but not brown, about 5 minutes. Combine eggs and milk; add to skillet. Cook till eggs are set throughout but still moist, 5 to 8 minutes, folding eggs over with wide spatula so uncooked part goes to bottom. Makes 6 servings.

Jiffy Ham Special

½ cup chopped onion
¼ cup chopped green pepper
2 tablespoons margarine or butter,
    melted
1 16-ounce can tomatoes, cut up
1½ cups cubed fully cooked ham
1½ cups water
¾ cup long grain rice
½ cup chili sauce
½ teaspoon salt
½ teaspoon Worcestershire sauce
    Dash pepper

• • •

Parsley

In 10-inch skillet cook chopped onion and green pepper in melted margarine or butter till vegetables are tender but not brown. Add undrained tomatoes, ham, water, uncooked rice, chili sauce, salt, Worcestershire sauce, and pepper. Cover and simmer 25 to 30 minutes, stirring once or twice. Trim ham mixture with parsley. Makes 6 servings.

Ham and Cheese Bake

Eggs, cheese, and ham make this recipe nutritious as well as appetizing—

3 tablespoons finely chopped onion
1 tablespoon margarine or butter,
    melted

• • •

3 beaten eggs
1½ cups milk
¾ cup finely crushed saltine crackers
    (about 20 crackers)
1½ cups finely chopped fully cooked ham
¾ cup shredded sharp American cheese
    (3 ounces)
    Dash pepper

In medium saucepan cook the chopped onion in margarine or butter till onion is tender but not brown. Combine the beaten eggs, milk, and crushed crackers. Add chopped ham, cheese, onion mixture, and pepper; mix well. Turn into a 9-inch pie plate. Bake at 350° till a knife inserted just off-center comes out clean, 30 to 35 minutes. Makes 4 to 6 servings.

Top Left: Make the most of ham by serving *Baked Ham Shank* (see recipe, page 38). By planning ahead you can use the extra meat in casseroles, patties, soups, and salads.

Bottom Left: *Curry-Ham-Rice Salad* (see recipe, page 38) is ideal for luncheons on hot summer afternoons. It features apples, ham, rice, and curry powder tossed with salad dressing.

Top Right: Bowls of steaming chowder are always a family favorite. Serve *Cauliflower-Ham Chowder* (see recipe, page 38) and you'll find everyone coming back for more.

Bottom Right: For a main dish in a hurry, try *Glazed Ham Patties* (see recipe, page 38). These patties are made from ham, bread crumbs, and celery. The glaze is apple jelly.

Acorn-Ham Bake

3 medium acorn squash
Salt
2 tablespoons margarine or butter

• • •

1 beaten egg
¼ cup milk
⅔ cup coarsely crushed saltine
    crackers (15 crackers)
¼ cup packed brown sugar
1 medium apple, peeled and chopped
¼ cup chopped onion
2 teaspoons prepared mustard
Dash pepper
1 pound ground fully cooked ham

Cut the squash in half lengthwise; remove the seeds. Place squash, cut side down, in a shallow baking pan. Bake at 350° till tender, about 45 minutes. Turn squash over. Salt each half lightly; dot with margarine or butter. Combine the beaten egg, milk, saltine crackers, brown sugar, chopped apple, chopped onion, prepared mustard, and pepper.

Add the ground ham; mix well. Fill the squash shells with the ham mixture. Continue baking till the ham mixture is heated through, about 20 minutes. Makes 6 servings.

Ham and Corn Supper

1 10½-ounce can condensed cream of
    celery soup
¼ cup milk
1 8¾-ounce can whole kernel corn,
    drained
1 cup chopped fully cooked ham
¼ cup chopped celery
¼ cup sliced pitted ripe olives
1 beaten egg
Basic Biscuits (see recipe,
    page 21)

Blend the soup and milk together. Stir in drained corn, ham, chopped celery, and the ripe olives. Heat the mixture through. Stir a moderate amount of hot mixture into beaten egg. Return to hot mixture. Cook over low heat till thickened, 1 to 2 minutes. Serve over the hot biscuits. Makes 4 servings.

Ham and Cheese Lasagne

6 lasagne noodles (about 6 ounces)
¼ cup chopped onion
¼ cup chopped green pepper
2 tablespoons margarine or butter
3 tablespoons all-purpose flour
1¾ cups milk
1 cup shredded Swiss cheese
    (4 ounces)
2 cups finely chopped fully cooked ham
1 3-ounce can chopped mushrooms,
    drained
Paprika

Cook lasagne noodles in boiling salted water just till tender, 15 to 20 minutes; drain. Rinse with cold water; drain. In medium saucepan cook onion and green pepper in margarine or butter till tender; blend in flour. Add milk all at once. Cook and stir till thickened and bubbly. Stir in Swiss cheese till melted. Stir in ham and mushrooms. Arrange *half* the noodles in greased 10x6x2-inch baking dish; spread with *half* the ham mixture. Repeat layers. Sprinkle with paprika. Bake, covered, at 375° till heated through, about 25 minutes. Let the lasagne stand 15 minutes before serving. Makes 6 servings.

Pineapple-Ham Cups

1 13¼-ounce can pineapple tidbits
2 tablespoons packed brown sugar
2 beaten eggs
1 cup soft bread crumbs
¼ cup finely chopped onion
Dash pepper
1 pound ground fully cooked ham

Drain the pineapple, reserving 3 tablespoons syrup. Place 6 tidbits in the bottom of *each* of six 6-ounce custard cups. Chop remaining tidbits; set aside. Sprinkle *1 teaspoon* brown sugar over the pineapple in *each* custard cup. Combine eggs, reserved syrup, bread crumbs, chopped onion, chopped pineapple, and pepper; add the ham and mix well. Divide ham mixture into 6 parts and fill custard cups. Bake at 350° for 20 to 25 minutes. Unmold ham cups to serve. Makes 4 servings.

Ham Soufflé in Pepper Cups

    6 large green peppers
    3 tablespoons margarine or butter
    3 tablespoons all-purpose flour
    ¾ cup milk
    ¾ cup shredded Swiss cheese
       (3 ounces)
    1 cup finely chopped fully cooked ham
    3 eggs

Halve the green peppers lengthwise; remove seeds and pulp. Cook the peppers in boiling salted water for 5 minutes. Drain the cooked peppers well; set aside. In medium saucepan melt the margarine or butter; stir in the flour. Add milk; cook and stir till very thick. Add shredded cheese; stir till cheese melts. Remove the cheese mixture from heat; stir in the ham. Separate the eggs.

    Beat egg yolks till thick and lemon-colored. Slowly stir cheese mixture into yolks; cool slightly. Beat the egg whites till stiff, but not dry peaks form. Gradually fold the cheese-yolk mixture into the egg whites; spoon mixture into pepper halves. Place in shallow baking pan with ½ inch water in pan. Bake at 375° for 25 to 30 minutes. Serves 6.

Corn Bread-Topped Ham Loaf

    2 beaten eggs
    ⅔ cup milk
    1 cup soft bread crumbs (1¼ slices
       bread)
    ¼ cup chopped onion
    2 pounds ground fully cooked ham
    ½ cup apricot preserves
    1 8-ounce package corn muffin mix

Combine beaten eggs, milk, soft bread crumbs, and chopped onion. Add the ground ham; mix well. Pat mixture into a 12x7½x2-inch baking dish. Bake at 350° for 30 minutes. Remove from oven; drain off any excess fat. Spread the apricot preserves over top of ham loaf. Increase the oven temperature to 400°. Prepare the corn muffin mix according to package directions; pour over the apricot preserves. Bake at 400° till corn bread layer is done, 20 to 25 minutes. Makes 8 servings.

Ham-Stuffed Cabbage Rolls

    1 cup narrow noodles
    ½ of a 10-ounce package frozen
       peas and carrots (1 cup)
  10 large cabbage leaves
    1 10¾-ounce can condensed cream of
       mushroom soup
    ½ cup milk
    1 pound ground fully cooked ham
    ¼ cup chopped onion
    1 beaten egg

Cook noodles and the peas and carrots according to individual package directions; drain. Combine and set aside. In a large saucepan cook cabbage leaves in boiling water for 5 minutes. Blend soup and milk; heat. Combine *1⅓ cups* of the soup mixture, the ham, noodle mixture, onion, and egg. Spoon *⅓ cup* ham mixture onto each cabbage leaf; fold in sides and roll ends over the meat. Place rolls in 12x7½x2-inch baking dish; pour the remaining soup mixture atop. Cover and bake at 325° for 1 hour. Makes 5 servings.

Ham-Turkey Pie

    ¼ cup margarine or butter
    5 tablespoons all-purpose flour
    ¼ teaspoon pepper
    2 cups chicken broth
    1 cup chopped fully cooked ham
    1 cup chopped cooked turkey
    ½ cup chopped mushrooms
    ¼ cup chopped green onion
    3 tablespoons snipped parsley
      Rice Shell

Melt margarine; blend in flour and pepper. Add broth all at once. Cook over medium heat, stirring constantly, till mixture thickens and bubbles. Add ham, turkey, mushrooms, onion, and parsley; mix well. Pour into prepared Rice Shell. Bake at 350° for 40 minutes. Let stand about 5 minutes. Serves 6.

Rice Shell: Thoroughly combine 2½ cups cooked long grain rice, 2 beaten eggs, ¼ cup melted margarine or butter, and ⅛ teaspoon pepper. Press the rice mixture firmly into an ungreased 9-inch pie plate.

Make the most of pork

Take advantage of the meat department's next special on pork by purchasing a lean roast from the blade end of the loin. Make your meat dollar stretch by buying a roast large enough for two meals. After serving the roast at one meal, refrigerate or freeze the remaining cooked pork to use in recipes such as Jiffy Pork Stew or Cranberry-Pork Bake.

Pork Blade Roast

Sprinkle one 3- to 4-pound pork blade roast with salt and pepper. Insert meat thermometer in center of thickest muscle, making sure not to touch bone. Place roast, fat side up, on a rack in shallow roasting pan. Do not cover, add water, or baste. (Meat browns as it cooks.) Roast at 325° till meat thermometer registers 170°, 2¼ to 2¾ hours. Let meat stand 15 minutes before carving. Plan on 3 servings per pound of meat as purchased.

Jiffy Pork Stew

  1 cup shredded carrot
  ½ cup chopped onion
  ¼ cup chopped green pepper
  3 tablespoons margarine or butter
1½ cups water
  ½ cup Creamy Chicken Gravy Base (see
     recipe, page 18)
  ¾ teaspoon salt
  ¼ teaspoon ground sage
  ⅛ teaspoon pepper
    Few drops bottled hot pepper sauce
  2 cups cubed cooked pork
  2 cups cubed cooked potatoes

In medium saucepan cook carrot, onion, and green pepper in margarine or butter till tender but not brown. Stir in water, Creamy Chicken Gravy Base, salt, sage, pepper, and hot pepper sauce. Add pork and potatoes. Bring to boiling; reduce heat. Cook and stir till mixture is heated through, about 10 minutes. Makes 4 servings.

Apple and Pork Casserole

  ¼ cup chopped onion
  1 tablespoon shortening
  1 10½-ounce can chicken
    gravy
  3 tablespoons packed brown sugar
  ¼ teaspoon ground cinnamon
  3 cups cubed cooked pork
  2 tart apples, chopped
    Packaged instant mashed potatoes
    (enough for 4 servings)
  ¼ cup milk
    Dash pepper
  1 beaten egg
  ½ cup shredded American cheese
    (2 ounces)

In saucepan cook onion in shortening till tender. Stir in gravy, sugar, and cinnamon; add pork and apples. Spoon into 8x1½-inch round baking dish. Prepare potatoes according to package directions, *except use ¼ cup milk and dash pepper.* Blend egg into potatoes. Spoon in 6 mounds on top of pork mixture. Bake at 350° for 25 minutes. Sprinkle cheese atop; bake 5 minutes more. Serves 6.

Creamy Pork and Sauerkraut

  1 cup chopped onion
  2 tablespoons cooking oil
  2 cups cubed cooked pork
  1 16-ounce can sauerkraut, drained
    and rinsed
  ¼ cup water
  1 teaspoon paprika
  ½ teaspoon salt
    • • •
  1 cup dairy sour cream

Cook chopped onion in hot cooking oil till tender but not brown. Add cubed pork, sauerkraut, water, paprika, and salt. Cover and simmer till flavors are blended, about 20 minutes. Stir in sour cream. Heat through, *but do not boil.* Makes 4 servings.

Cranberry-Pork Bake

    1 8-ounce can whole cranberry sauce
    2 tablespoons light corn syrup
    1 17-ounce can sweet potatoes,
        drained
    2 tablespoons margarine or butter,
        melted
    1 tablespoon packed brown sugar
    1 teaspoon salt
    ¼ teaspoon ground ginger
    2 cups chopped cooked pork

Combine cranberry sauce and corn syrup in mixing bowl; set aside. With electric mixer beat sweet potatoes with margarine or butter, brown sugar, salt, and ginger till well blended. Stir in pork. Turn into a 1-quart casserole. Bake at 350° for 35 minutes. Spread with cranberry mixture; bake 5 to 10 minutes more. Makes 4 servings.

Pork Pie

    2 cups diced carrots
    ¼ cup chopped onion
    ½ cup milk
    ¼ cup all-purpose flour
    1 10½-ounce can chicken gravy
    2½ to 3 cups cubed cooked pork
    2 tablespoons sliced pimiento-stuffed
        green olives
    1 cup Basic Biscuit Mix (see recipe,
        page 20)
    ¼ teaspoon rubbed sage

In saucepan cook carrots and onion in ½ cup water for 10 minutes. Do not drain. Blend milk into flour; mix with chicken gravy. Stir into carrots. Cook and stir till slightly thickened and bubbly. Stir in pork, olives, and dash pepper. Bring to boiling. Turn into 2-quart casserole. Combine Basic Biscuit Mix and sage. Add ⅓ cup water all at once. Stir with fork just till dough follows fork around bowl. Knead dough 10 to 12 strokes on a surface sprinkled lightly with biscuit mix. Roll or pat dough into a 9-inch circle. Cut into 6 wedges. Arrange on top of *hot* mixture, leaving spaces between wedges. Bake at 450° for 15 minutes. Makes 6 servings.

Pork Florentine

    2 10-ounce packages frozen chopped
        spinach
    1 10½-ounce can condensed cream of
        chicken soup
    ¼ cup shredded Swiss cheese (1 ounce)
    2 tablespoons salad dressing or
        mayonnaise
    1 teaspoon lemon juice
    ½ teaspoon Worcestershire sauce
    1½ cups chopped cooked pork
    1 cup soft bread crumbs
    2 tablespoons margarine or butter,
        melted

Cook spinach according to package directions, *except use unsalted water;* drain. Mix soup, cheese, salad dressing, lemon juice, and Worcestershire; bring to boiling. Blend ¾ *cup* sauce with spinach. Pat spinach mixture into 6 individual casseroles. Top with pork. Spoon remaining sauce over. Combine crumbs and margarine; sprinkle atop casseroles. Bake at 350° for 25 minutes. Makes 6 servings.

Barbecued Pork Sandwich

    ½ cup chopped onion
    ¼ cup chopped celery
    1 clove garlic, minced
    2 tablespoons margarine or butter
    1 cup chili sauce
    ½ cup water
    2 tablespoons packed brown sugar
    2 tablespoons vinegar
    2 tablespoons Worcestershire sauce
    ¾ teaspoon chili powder
    ¼ teaspoon salt
        Dash pepper
    12 thin slices cooked pork
            • • •
    6 hamburger buns, split and toasted

In medium skillet cook onion, celery, and garlic in margarine or butter till tender but not brown. Stir in chili sauce, water, brown sugar, vinegar, Worcestershire, chili powder, salt, and pepper. Simmer, covered, 10 to 15 minutes. Add pork; heat through. Serve meat on buns with sauce. Makes 6 sandwiches.

Top Left: Make the most of pork by fixing *Pork Blade Roast* (see recipe, page 44). Using the planned-over meat in casseroles and in sandwiches shortens meal preparation time.

Bottom Left: Served in attractive individual casseroles, *Pork Florentine* (see recipe, page 45) features spinach, cream of chicken soup, Swiss cheese, bread crumbs, and cooked pork.

Top Right: *Cranberry-Pork Bake* (see recipe, page 45) is a meal in one dish. This tasty casserole combines sweet potatoes with cooked pork, ginger, and cranberry sauce.

Bottom Right: Serving *Apple and Pork Casserole* (see recipe, page 44) is an economical way to use leftover pork. This hearty mixture is topped with mashed potatoes and cheese.

Canadian Pork Pie

1 pound ground pork
1 cup water
½ cup finely chopped onion
½ cup fine dry bread crumbs
¾ teaspoon salt
  Dash pepper
  Dash ground sage
  Dash ground nutmeg
  Pastry for 2-crust 9-inch pie
    (see recipe, page 17)

Brown the pork in skillet; drain off excess fat. Add water, onion, crumbs, and seasonings. Simmer, covered, 30 minutes, stirring occasionally. Line 9-inch pie plate with pastry. Turn meat mixture into crust. Adjust top crust; seal. Cut slits in top for escape of steam. Bake at 400° till crust is golden brown, about 35 minutes. Makes 6 servings.

Dressed-Up Pork Steaks

4 pork shoulder steaks, cut
    ½ inch thick
4 slices white bread, toasted
1 beaten egg
2 teaspoons grated orange peel
½ cup orange juice
½ cup finely chopped celery
¼ cup finely chopped onion
½ teaspoon poultry seasoning
¼ teaspoon salt
  Paprika

Trim excess fat from pork steaks; cook trimmings in skillet till 1 tablespoon fat accumulates. Discard trimmings. Brown the steaks in hot fat. Sprinkle with salt and pepper. Cut toasted bread in small cubes. Combine egg, orange peel, and juice; add bread cubes, celery, onion, poultry seasoning, and salt. Shape orange dressing into mounds by pressing bread mixture into a ⅓ cup measure. Place a mound of dressing on each steak. Pour ¼ cup water in bottom of skillet. Cover and simmer 30 minutes. Remove cover and cook 15 minutes longer. If necessary, add a little more water. Sprinkle dressing mounds with paprika. Makes 4 servings.

Seasoned Pork Chop Dinner

ENTERTAINING SPECIAL

3 cups farfalle (butterfly-
    shaped pasta)
1 16-ounce can tomatoes
½ teaspoon salt
¼ teaspoon dried thyme, crushed
6 pork shoulder chops, cut ½ inch
    thick
½ cup chopped onion
1 beef bouillon cube
½ teaspoon salt
¼ teaspoon dried marjoram, crushed
½ green pepper, cut in rings
  Paprika

In a saucepan cook farfalle in boiling salted water just till tender, 10 to 12 minutes; drain. Drain tomatoes, reserving ¾ cup juice. Cut tomatoes into quarters; stir into farfalle along with the ½ teaspoon salt and the thyme. Place in 12x7½x2-inch baking dish. Trim fat from chops; cook trimmings in skillet till 2 tablespoons fat accumulate. Discard trimmings. Brown the chops in hot fat. Arrange chops over farfalle. Sprinkle chops with onion. In small saucepan combine reserved tomato juice, the bouillon cube, ½ teaspoon salt, the marjoram, and dash pepper. Cook and stir till bouillon cube is dissolved; pour over chops. Cover and bake at 350° for 1 hour. Remove cover; place green pepper rings atop chops. Cover and bake till green pepper is tender, about 15 minutes more. Sprinkle with paprika. Makes 6 servings.

Add just the right seasoning

Spark up ground meat dishes by adding different herb combinations. Pork blends well with clove, garlic, ginger, mustard, oregano, sage, or thyme. Seasonings often used with beef are basil, chili powder, cumin, curry, dill, garlic, marjoram, mustard, oregano, or thyme. Try ham with allspice, cinnamon, clove, ginger, or mustard. And add mint, oregano, rosemary, savory, or thyme to lamb.

Hungarian-Style Pork Chops

**6 pork rib chops, cut 1 inch
   thick
2 tablespoons cooking oil
½ cup chopped onion
2 cloves garlic, minced
1 tablespoon all-purpose flour
1 tablespoon paprika
1 cup chicken broth
1 tablespoon caraway seed
⅛ teaspoon cayenne
1 27-ounce can sauerkraut, rinsed
   and well drained
1 cup dairy sour cream**

Sprinkle pork chops with salt and pepper. In a large skillet brown the chops in hot cooking oil; remove chops from skillet. In same skillet cook onion and garlic till tender but not brown. Add flour and paprika. Stir in broth, caraway seed, and cayenne; mix well. Bring to boiling; stir in sauerkraut. Return chops to skillet. Cover and simmer over low heat till meat is tender, about 50 minutes. Remove chops to warm platter. Stir sour cream into sauerkraut mixture; heat through *but do not boil*. Makes 6 servings.

Burritos

**1 pound ground pork
2 tablespoons all-purpose flour
1 16-ounce can tomatoes, cut up
½ cup chopped onion
2 canned green chili peppers, seeded
   and chopped
1 small clove garlic, minced
12 canned tortillas *or* frozen
   tortillas, thawed**

In skillet cook pork till browned; drain off excess fat. Stir in flour, 1 teaspoon salt, and dash pepper. Add undrained tomatoes, onion, chili peppers, and garlic. Cook and stir over medium heat till thickened and bubbly. Reduce heat; simmer 10 minutes. Place tortillas on baking sheet. Bake at 350° for 4 or 5 minutes. To serve, spoon about ¼ cup pork mixture in the center of each tortilla; fold in all sides. Makes 12 burritos.

Pork and Eggplant Bake

**1 pound ground pork
¼ cup chopped onion
1 clove garlic, minced
2 cups Marinara Sauce (see recipe,
   page 15)
1 teaspoon dried oregano, crushed
1 teaspoon dried basil, crushed
1 eggplant, peeled (about 1¼ pounds)
¼ cup cooking oil
½ cup grated Parmesan cheese
1 cup shredded mozzarella cheese
   (4 ounces)**

Cook pork, onion, and garlic till meat is browned. Add next 3 ingredients. Cook and stir 5 minutes. Slice eggplant ¼ inch thick. Brush slices with oil and cook in skillet till golden on both sides. Place half the eggplant in bottom of a greased 12x7½x2-inch baking dish. Sprinkle with *half* the Parmesan; cover with *half* the meat sauce. Repeat layers. Sprinkle with mozzarella. Bake at 350° for 15 minutes. Makes 6 servings.

Cherry-Crowned Pork Loaf

**2 beaten eggs
½ cup milk
1½ cups soft rye bread crumbs
2 teaspoons prepared mustard
½ teaspoon poultry seasoning
1 pound ground pork
1 pound ground fully cooked ham
1 21-ounce can cherry pie filling
1 tablespoon lemon juice
½ teaspoon ground cinnamon
   Dash ground cloves**

Combine eggs, milk, bread crumbs, mustard, poultry seasoning, ¼ teaspoon salt, and ¼ teaspoon pepper. Add ground pork and ham; mix well. Pat into a greased 9x5x3-inch loaf pan. Bake at 350° for 1 hour 20 minutes. Meanwhile, in saucepan combine pie filling, lemon juice, ground cinnamon, cloves, and 2 tablespoons water. Keep sauce warm. Drain off pan juices from meat loaf. Invert the loaf onto warm serving platter. Serve some sauce atop loaf; pass the remaining sauce. Serves 8.

Orange-Glazed Ribs

Win your guests' approval by serving them these country-style ribs (see photo, page 4)—

> 4 pounds pork country-style ribs
> • • •
> 1½ teaspoons grated orange peel or tangerine peel
> 1 cup orange juice or tangerine juice
> ½ cup light corn syrup
> 3 tablespoons soy sauce
> ¾ teaspoon ground ginger

Place ribs, meaty side down, in shallow roasting pan. Roast at 450° for 30 minutes. Meanwhile, prepare glaze. Combine the orange peel and juice, light corn syrup, soy sauce, and ginger; mix thoroughly. Remove ribs from oven; drain off excess fat. Turn ribs meaty side up. Reduce oven temperature to 350°; continue roasting for 30 minutes. Drain. Roast 30 minutes more, brush frequently with *half* of the orange glaze. Heat and pass remaining glaze. Garnish with orange quarters, if desired. Makes 6 servings.

Island Sweet-Sour Pork

> 1½ pounds boneless pork shoulder, cut in small cubes
> 1 tablespoon cooking oil
> 1 teaspoon salt
> Dash pepper
> 1 8½-ounce can pineapple tidbits
> ½ cup bottled barbecue sauce
> 1 tablespoon quick-cooking tapioca
> • • •
> 1 medium green pepper, cut in strips
> Hot cooked rice

In medium skillet brown the pork in hot cooking oil. Season meat with salt and pepper. Drain the pineapple, reserving the pineapple syrup. Add water to the syrup to make ¾ cup liquid. Stir the syrup, barbecue sauce, and tapioca into the browned meat. Cover the skillet and simmer till meat is tender, about 45 minutes. Add the drained pineapple and green pepper strips; heat the mixture thoroughly. Serve the pork mixture over hot cooked rice. Makes 6 servings.

Pork Marengo

Tender pieces of pork enhanced by vegetables, marjoram, and thyme (see photo, page 22)—

> 2 pounds boneless pork shoulder, cut in 1-inch cubes
> ½ cup chopped onion
> 2 tablespoons cooking oil
> 1 16-ounce can tomatoes, cut up
> ½ cup water
> 1 teaspoon instant chicken bouillon granules
> 1 teaspoon dried marjoram, crushed
> ¾ teaspoon salt
> ¼ teaspoon dried thyme, crushed
> Dash pepper
> 1 3-ounce can chopped mushrooms, drained
> ¼ cup cold water
> 3 tablespoons all-purpose flour
> Hot cooked rice

In skillet brown the pork cubes and chopped onion in hot cooking oil. Stir in undrained tomatoes, the ½ cup water, bouillon granules, marjoram, salt, thyme, and pepper. Cover and simmer the mixture till pork is tender, about 60 minutes. Add the mushrooms to the pork. Slowly blend the ¼ cup cold water into flour. Stir into the pork mixture; cook and stir till thickened and bubbly. Serve over hot cooked rice. Makes 8 to 10 servings.

Country Dinner

> 1 1½-pound smoked pork shoulder roll
> 1 16-ounce can sauerkraut, drained
> 2 cups apple juice
> 1 large bay leaf
> • • •
> 6 medium potatoes, peeled
> 6 small onions
> 6 small carrots, quartered

Place the pork shoulder roll in a 5-quart Dutch oven; add drained sauerkraut, apple juice, and bay leaf. Cover; simmer 1 hour. Add the potatoes, onions, and carrots. Simmer, covered, till tender, about 1 hour more. Remove meat and vegetables to warm serving platter. Makes 6 servings.

Chinese Pork Skillet

  3 tablespoons cornstarch
  1 tablespoon soy sauce
  1 pound boneless pork shoulder, cut
    in ½-inch cubes
  2 tablespoons cooking oil
  1 16-ounce can mixed Chinese
    vegetables, drained
  1 8½-ounce can pineapple tidbits,
    drained
  1 cup water
  ⅓ cup chopped onion
  ¼ cup packed brown sugar
  ¼ cup vinegar
  2 teaspoons instant chicken bouillon
    granules
  1 clove garlic, minced
  1 5½-ounce can chow mein noodles

In small, deep bowl combine cornstarch, soy sauce, ¼ teaspoon salt, and ⅛ teaspoon pepper. Add pork; stir to coat. Brown in hot oil. Add remaining ingredients except chow mein noodles. Cover and simmer 20 to 25 minutes. Serve over chow mein noodles. Serves 4 or 5.

Curried Pork

  1 pound boneless pork shoulder, cut
    in ¾-inch cubes
  ⅓ cup all-purpose flour
  2 tablespoons shortening
  1 large onion, sliced
  ½ cup chopped green pepper
  1 15-ounce can tomato sauce
  2 teaspoons curry powder
  1 clove garlic, minced
  1 10-ounce package frozen peas and
    carrots
    Hot cooked rice *or* noodles

Coat pork with flour. Brown the meat in the hot shortening. Add onion and pepper; cook till tender. Combine tomato sauce, curry powder, garlic, 1½ cups water, 1 teaspoon salt, and ¼ teaspoon pepper. Pour over meat. Cover and cook over low heat till meat is tender, 1 hour. Add the peas and carrots. Cook till vegetables are tender, 15 to 20 minutes more. Serve over rice or noodles. Serves 4.

Pork and Vegetable Stew

  2 pounds boneless pork shoulder, cut
    in 1-inch cubes
  ⅓ cup all-purpose flour
  2 teaspoons salt
  ½ teaspoon ground sage
  3 tablespoons shortening
  1 clove garlic, minced
  1 bay leaf
  4 medium carrots, cut in ½-inch pieces
  3 medium potatoes, peeled and sliced
  1 10-ounce package frozen lima beans

Trim excess fat from meat. Combine flour, *1 teaspoon* of the salt, sage, and ¼ teaspoon pepper. Coat meat with the flour mixture. Brown in hot shortening; pour off fat. Add garlic, bay leaf, and 3 cups water. Cover tightly and simmer 40 minutes. Add vegetables and remaining 1 teaspoon salt; continue cooking till vegetables are tender, 15 to 20 minutes. Remove bay leaf. Season stew with salt and pepper to taste. Serves 8.

Pork Stroganoff

  1 pound chopped boneless pork shoulder
  1 tablespoon cooking oil
  ½ cup chopped onion
  1 3-ounce can chopped mushrooms,
    drained
  1 clove garlic, minced
  1 tablespoon instant beef bouillon
    granules
  1 teaspoon dried dillweed
  ½ cup dairy sour cream
  ¼ cup dry white wine
  2 tablespoons all-purpose flour
    Hot buttered noodles
    Snipped parsley

In medium saucepan brown the pork in hot oil. Drain off fat. Add onion, mushrooms, garlic, bouillon granules, dillweed, 1 cup water, and ⅛ teaspoon pepper to pork. Cover and simmer till pork is tender, 40 to 45 minutes. Blend sour cream, wine, and flour. Add mixture to skillet; cook and stir till hot, *but do not boil.* Serve over noodles. Garnish with parsley. Makes 6 servings.

Make the most of poultry

Large whole turkeys and roasting chickens are real bargains because the proportion of meat to bone is high. For maximum savings, buy the largest bird you can cook and store. Prepare the bird as a roast, then refrigerate or wrap and freeze the leftovers. Use this planned-over meat for recipes such as Turkey au Gratin, Turkey-Biscuit Ring, or Curried Turkey Salad. Then, use the chicken or turkey frame for soups such as Turkey Frame Soup.

Roast Turkey or Chicken

Rinse ready-to-cook turkey or chicken; pat dry. Sprinkle cavity of bird with salt. Stuff, if desired. Tuck legs under band of skin or tie legs to tail. Place bird, breast side up, on rack in shallow roasting pan. Rub skin with cooking oil. Insert meat thermometer in center of inside thigh muscle, not touching bone. Cover loosely with foil (for chicken, roast uncovered). Roast according to chart below. During last 45 minutes, cut band of skin or string between legs and tail. Continue roasting till drumstick moves easily and meat thermometer registers 180° to 185°. Let stand 15 minutes before carving. Plan on 2 servings per pound of bird as purchased.

Poultry Roasting Chart			
Poultry	Ready-To-Cook Weight	Oven Temp.	Roasting Time Stuffed and Unstuffed
Turkey	6-8 lbs.	325°	3½-4 hrs.
	8-12 lbs.	325°	4-4½ hrs.
	12-16 lbs.	325°	4½-5½ hrs.
	16-20 lbs.	325°	5½-6½ hrs.
	20-24 lbs.	325°	6½-7½ hrs.
Chicken	1½-2 lbs.	375°	¾-1 hr.
	2-2½ lbs.	375°	1-1¼ hrs.
	2½-3 lbs.	375°	1¼-1½ hrs.
	3-4 lbs.	375°	1½-2 hrs.

Turkey-Biscuit Ring

¼ cup finely chopped onion
¼ cup finely chopped celery
1 tablespoon margarine or butter
1 10½-ounce can condensed cream of chicken soup
2 cups finely chopped cooked turkey
2 cups Basic Biscuit Mix (see recipe, page 20)
½ cup yellow cornmeal
2 tablespoons snipped parsley
¼ cup milk
2 tablespoons chopped canned pimiento

Cook onion and celery in margarine till tender. Add ½ *cup* soup and dash pepper. Stir in turkey; set aside. Blend next 3 ingredients and ¾ cup water. Stir till dough follows fork around bowl. On floured surface knead dough 10 to 12 times; roll or pat to a 12x8-inch rectangle. Spread turkey mixture over dough. Roll as for jelly roll, starting at long end. Form into ring on greased baking sheet; pinch to seal. Make cuts at 1½-inch intervals to, but not through bottom of ring. Bake at 400° for 20 to 25 minutes. Combine the remaining soup, milk, and pimiento. Heat through. Serve with ring. Serves 6 to 8.

Curried Turkey Salad

2 small cantaloupes
2 cups cubed cooked turkey
1 cup seedless green grapes, halved
½ cup sliced celery
¾ cup salad dressing or mayonnaise
½ cup dairy sour cream
2 teaspoons soy sauce
¾ teaspoon curry powder

Using sawtooth cut, halve melons; remove seeds. Scoop out pulp; cube. Mix melon, turkey, grapes, and celery. Spoon mixture into melon halves. Combine remaining ingredients and ¼ teaspoon salt. Pour over mixture in melon halves. Makes 4 servings.

Turkey au Gratin

    2 cups medium noodles
    ½ cup chopped onion
    1 tablespoon margarine or butter
    1 cup White Sauce Mix (see recipe,
        page 19)
    1½ cups diced cooked turkey
    1 3-ounce can chopped mushrooms,
        drained
    ½ cup shredded American cheese
    3 tablespoons sliced pimiento-stuffed
        green olives
    1 tablespoon lemon juice
    ½ cup finely crushed rich round
        crackers (12 crackers)
    1 tablespoon margarine, melted

Cook noodles according to package directions. Drain and set aside. Cook onion in the 1 tablespoon margarine till tender. Prepare White Sauce Mix, following recipe directions for a medium white sauce. Mix together the onion, prepared White Sauce Mix, turkey, mushrooms, cheese, olives, and lemon juice; fold into noodles. Spoon mixture into a 1½-quart casserole. Combine cracker crumbs and melted margarine. Sprinkle over casserole. Bake, uncovered, at 350° till heated through, 40 to 45 minutes. Serves 4 or 5.

Turkey-Tomato Bake

    ½ cup chopped onion
    ½ cup chopped celery
    1 tablespoon margarine or butter
    1 17-ounce can whole kernel corn,
        drained
    1½ cups chopped cooked turkey
    1 10¾-ounce can condensed tomato soup
    ⅓ cup catsup
    ¼ cup shredded American cheese
    1 9-ounce package frozen French-fried
        crinkle-cut potatoes

In a skillet cook onion and celery in margarine till vegetables are tender but not brown. Add the corn, turkey, soup, catsup, and cheese. Turn into an 8x8x2-inch baking dish. Arrange potatoes over top. Bake, uncovered, at 425° for 25 minutes. Serves 6.

Turkey Frame Soup

    5 quarts water
    1 meaty turkey frame
    1 onion, quartered
    4 teaspoons salt
    8 cups fresh vegetables*
    1 16-ounce can tomatoes, cut up
    1 teaspoon dried thyme, crushed
    ½ teaspoon dried oregano, crushed
        Homemade Noodles (see recipe, page
            17) or packaged noodles

In Dutch oven combine water, turkey frame, onion, and salt. Simmer, covered, 1½ hours. Remove frame and onion; cool frame. Remove meat from bones. Discard bones and onion. Add the turkey meat, fresh vegetables, undrained tomatoes, thyme, and oregano to the broth. Bring mixture to boiling; cover. Simmer 45 minutes. Add Homemade Noodles; boil 15 minutes more. Makes 4 quarts.
  *Any combination of sliced celery or carrot, chopped onion or rutabaga, sliced mushrooms, chopped broccoli, or cauliflowerets.

Tokyo Turkey Toss

    2 cups cubed cooked turkey
    1 16-ounce can bean sprouts, drained
    1 cup cooked rice, chilled
    1 cup chopped celery
    1 cup coarsely shredded carrot
    2 tablespoons chopped green pepper
    ¼ cup French salad dressing
    2 tablespoons soy sauce
    ¼ teaspoon salt
        Dash pepper
    ½ cup salad dressing or mayonnaise
    ½ cup slivered almonds, toasted
        Lettuce cups

In a bowl combine cooked turkey, drained bean sprouts, rice, celery, shredded carrot, and green pepper. Mix together French salad dressing, soy sauce, salt, and pepper. Toss with turkey mixture. Chill.
  Just before serving, stir in salad dressing or mayonnaise and slivered almonds. Toss the mixture thoroughly. Serve turkey mixture in lettuce cups. Makes 6 servings.

Top Left: Make the most of poultry by serving *Roast Turkey or Chicken* (see recipe, page 52). Then, make the leftovers disappear in a jiffy by using them in casseroles, salads, and soups.

Bottom Left: For your next luncheon try *Curried Turkey Salads* (see recipe, page 52). This attractive main dish salad is a blend of cantaloupe, turkey, grapes, and curry powder.

Top Right: Don't discard that leftover turkey frame. Use it in *Turkey Frame Soup* (see recipe, page 53). This soup has a flavorful broth, homemade noodles, and lots of vegetables.

Bottom Right: If you are looking for something different, *Turkey-Biscuit Ring* (see recipe, page 52) is the answer. This recipe features a turkey filling and bread in one dish.

Turkey Hash—Oven-Style

    1½ cups coarsely ground cooked turkey
    1 cup cubed cooked potato
    1 5⅓-ounce can evaporated milk (⅔ cup)
    ¼ cup finely snipped parsley
    ¼ cup finely chopped onion
    1 teaspoon Worcestershire sauce
    ¼ teaspoon ground sage
    ¼ cup finely crushed saltine crackers
        (about 7 crackers)
    1 tablespoon margarine or butter,
        melted

Stir together first 7 ingredients, ½ teaspoon salt, and dash pepper. Turn into greased 1-quart casserole. Toss together crumbs and margarine or butter; sprinkle atop hash. Bake, uncovered, at 350° till heated through, about 30 minutes. Makes 4 servings.

Turkey-Sauced Spoon Bread

    Spoon Bread
    ½ cup chopped onion
    ¼ cup chopped green pepper
    1 clove garlic, minced
    1 tablespoon cooking oil
    1 15-ounce can tomato sauce
    1½ to 2 cups diced cooked turkey
    1 to 1½ teaspoons chili powder
    1 teaspoon sugar

Prepare Spoon Bread. Cook onion, pepper, and garlic in hot oil till tender but not brown. Stir in next 4 ingredients and ½ teaspoon salt. Simmer, covered, for 15 minutes. Serve over wedges of Spoon Bread. Serves 4 to 6.

Spoon Bread: In saucepan gradually stir ⅔ cup yellow cornmeal into 2 cups milk. Cook and stir till thickened. Add 1 cup shredded American cheese (4 ounces), 1 tablespoon margarine, ¾ teaspoon baking powder, ½ teaspoon salt, and ¼ teaspoon paprika. Stir till cheese melts and ingredients are blended. Gradually add a moderate amount of hot mixture to 2 beaten egg yolks; beat well and return to hot mixture. Beat 2 egg whites till stiff; fold into cornmeal mixture. Turn into a greased 9-inch pie plate. Bake at 350° for 40 to 45 minutes.

Cheesy Patty Cakes

    ½ cup finely chopped celery
    2 tablespoons margarine or butter
    1⅓ cups water
        Packaged instant mashed potatoes
        (enough for 4 servings)
    1 beaten egg
    ¼ cup shredded sharp American cheese
        (1 ounce)
    1 teaspoon instant minced onion
    1 teaspoon dried parsley flakes
        Dash pepper
    1 cup finely chopped cooked turkey
    ⅓ cup fine dry bread crumbs
        Cheese Sauce

In medium skillet cook celery in margarine till tender. Stir in water. Bring to boiling; stir in instant mashed potatoes, egg, cheese, onion, parsley, and pepper. Mix in turkey. Shape into 12 patties; coat with crumbs. Cook on hot greased griddle over medium heat about 2 minutes on each side. Serve patties with Cheese Sauce. Makes 4 servings.

Cheese Sauce: In small saucepan combine ¾ cup shredded sharp American cheese (3 ounces); ½ cup White Sauce Mix (see recipe, page 19); and ¾ cup cold water. Cook over low heat, stirring constantly, till the sauce is thickened and bubbly. Makes 1 cup.

Turkey-Sausage Skillet

    ½ pound bulk pork sausage
    ⅓ cup chopped onion
    ¼ cup chopped green pepper
    ¾ cup Creamy Chicken Gravy Base (see
        recipe, page 18)
    1 16-ounce can cut green beans, drained
    1½ cups diced cooked turkey
    2 tablespoons snipped parsley
        Basic Biscuits (see recipe, page 21)

In medium skillet cook sausage, onion, and green pepper till meat is browned and vegetables are tender; drain. Stir in Creamy Chicken Gravy Base and 2 cups water; cook and stir till mixture bubbles. Stir in beans, turkey, and parsley. Heat through. Serve on Basic Biscuits. Makes 6 servings.

Cranberry-Orange Chicken

    1 2½- to 3-pound ready-to-cook broiler-
        fryer chicken, cut up
    1 10½-ounce can condensed beef broth
    ¾ cup cranberry juice cocktail
    ¼ cup margarine or butter
    2 medium oranges, thinly sliced
    1 tablespoon cornstarch
    2 tablespoons sugar
    1 tablespoon vinegar

In saucepan combine chicken neck, giblets, and beef broth. Simmer, covered, for 1 hour; strain. Add cranberry cocktail to broth. Boil, uncovered, till liquid is reduced to 1 cup.

Brown remaining chicken pieces in *2 tablespoons* of the margarine. Place in a 12x 7½x2-inch baking dish. Sprinkle with salt. Bake at 350° for 25 minutes. Add orange slices to chicken pieces; bake 30 to 35 minutes more. To serve, blend cornstarch with 1 tablespoon cold water; stir into cranberry-broth mixture. Cook and stir till thickened. In saucepan melt the remaining 2 tablespoons margarine. Stir in sugar. Cook and stir till mixture thickens and bubbles. Add vinegar. Stir sugar mixture into cranberry sauce; heat through. Pass with chicken. Serves 4 or 5.

Chicken Custard

    1¾ cups milk
    2 teaspoons instant chicken bouillon
        granules
    2 beaten eggs
    ½ cup finely chopped cooked chicken
    4 rusks
        Jellied cranberry sauce, sliced

In saucepan heat milk; dissolve bouillon granules in milk. Stir a moderate amount of the hot mixture into eggs; return to remaining hot mixture. Divide chicken among four 6-ounce custard cups. Fill cups with egg mixture. Set in shallow baking pan on oven rack. Pour hot water into pan 1 inch deep. Bake at 325° till knife inserted off-center comes out clean, 40 to 45 minutes. Turn out and serve on rusks. Garnish with cranberry slices, cut into stars. Makes 4 servings.

Chicken and Dumplings

    1 5- to 6-pound ready-to-cook stewing
        chicken, cut up
    4 stalks celery with leaves
    1 carrot, sliced
    1 small onion, sliced
    2 sprigs parsley
    1 bay leaf
    2 teaspoons salt
    2 cups Basic Biscuit Mix (see recipe,
        page 20)
    ¼ cup snipped parsley
    ½ teaspoon poultry seasoning
    ⅔ cup milk
    ½ cup all-purpose flour

In large Dutch oven add enough water to chicken to cover. Add celery, carrot, onion, 2 sprigs parsley, bay leaf, salt, and ¼ teaspoon pepper. Cover; bring to boiling. Simmer till done, 1½ to 1¾ hours. In mixing bowl combine Basic Biscuit Mix, snipped parsley, and poultry seasoning. Add milk all at once. Stir till dough follows fork around bowl. Drop dough onto boiling chicken mixture, making 6 to 8 dumplings. Cover tightly; return to boiling. Simmer 15 to 20 minutes (don't lift cover). Remove dumplings and chicken to platter; keep warm.

For gravy: Strain broth; skim off fat. Measure 2½ cups broth into saucepan. Add 1 teaspoon salt and ⅛ teaspoon pepper. Slowly blend ½ cup cold water into the flour. Gradually add to broth, mixing well. Cook and stir till thickened and bubbly. Serve with chicken and dumplings. Makes 6 servings.

Add an attractive garnish

Make even the plainest main dish seem elegant by choosing the right garnish. For casseroles, use hard-cooked egg slices, sieved egg yolk, sliced pickle, or snipped parsley. For other meat dishes, choose from orange or lemon slices, carrot curls, bacon curls, tomato wedges, radish roses, or pimiento-stuffed green olives.

Chicken Crepes Elegante

1 beaten egg
1 cup milk
1 tablespoon margarine
    or butter, melted
1 cup all-purpose flour
6 tablespoons margarine or butter
6 tablespoons all-purpose flour
    Dash salt
3 cups milk
½ cup shredded sharp American cheese
    (2 ounces)
¼ cup dry white wine
1 3-ounce can sliced mushrooms,
    drained
2 cups finely chopped cooked chicken
1 10-ounce package frozen chopped
    broccoli, cooked and drained

For crepes: In mixing bowl combine egg, the 1 cup milk, and the 1 tablespoon margarine or butter. Add the 1 cup flour; beat till smooth. Lightly grease a 6-inch skillet; heat. Pour 2 tablespoons batter into skillet; lift pan and tilt from side to side till batter covers bottom. Return to heat; brown the crepe on *one side only.* Repeat this procedure, making 12 crepes in all. Set crepes aside.

For sauce: Melt the 6 tablespoons margarine or butter in a medium saucepan. Blend in the 6 tablespoons flour and salt. Add the 3 cups milk all at once. Cook, stirring constantly, till mixture thickens and bubbles. Stir in cheese and wine till cheese melts. Remove ½ *cup* of the sauce; set aside. Stir sliced mushrooms into remaining sauce.

For filling: Combine chicken, broccoli, and ½ cup reserved sauce. Spoon about ¼ cup filling on unbrowned side of each crepe. Roll up jelly-roll fashion. Arrange, seam side down, in chafing dish or crepe pan. Drizzle mushroom sauce over crepes. Cook, covered, over low heat till bubbly. Serves 6.

Company-perfect crepes

← *Chicken Crepes Elegante* will make a meal to be remembered. Filled with chicken and broccoli and topped with mushroom sauce, they will win praise from all your guests.

Chicken-Stuffing Scallop

2 cups Herb Stuffing Cubes
    (see recipe, page 16)
1½ cups diced cooked chicken
¼ cup margarine or butter
¼ cup all-purpose flour
2 teaspoons instant chicken bouillon
    granules
3 beaten eggs
    Paprika
½ cup milk
1 10¾-ounce can condensed Cheddar
    cheese soup
2 tablespoons chopped canned pimiento

Spread Herb Stuffing Cubes in a greased 10x 6x2-inch baking dish; top with chicken. In saucepan melt margarine or butter; blend in flour, bouillon granules, and dash pepper. Add 2 cups water. Cook and stir till thickened and bubbly. Gradually stir a moderate amount of hot mixture into eggs; return to remaining hot mixture. Pour over chicken. Sprinkle with paprika; cover with foil. Bake at 325° for 25 minutes. Uncover. Continue baking till knife inserted halfway between center and edge comes out clean, about 20 minutes more. Let stand 5 minutes before serving. In saucepan blend milk into soup; add pimiento. Cook and stir till heated through. Serve over chicken. Serves 6.

Chicken and Rice Balls

Cook ½ cup chopped celery and ¼ cup sliced green onion in 2 tablespoons margarine or butter till tender. Blend in 2 tablespoons all-purpose flour; add ¼ cup chicken broth. Cook and stir till thickened and bubbly. Stir in 2 cups cooked rice, 1½ cups diced cooked chicken, ½ cup shredded American cheese (2 ounces), 1 beaten egg, ½ teaspoon salt, ½ teaspoon chili powder, and ¼ teaspoon poultry seasoning. Form mixture into 12 balls; roll in ½ cup crushed cornflakes. Bake in 13x9x2-inch baking pan at 350° for 25 to 30 minutes. Heat one 10¾-ounce can condensed cream of mushroom soup, ¼ cup milk, and 2 tablespoons sliced green onion. Serve over chicken balls. Makes 4 servings.

Make the most of other meats

Mushroom-Sauced Chicken Livers

2 slices bacon
1 pound chicken livers, halved
1 16-ounce can cut green beans, drained
1½ cups bias-sliced celery
1 10¾-ounce can condensed cream of
    mushroom soup
2 tablespoons chopped canned pimiento
2 tablespoons grated Parmesan cheese

In skillet cook bacon till crisp; drain, reserving drippings. Crumble bacon and set aside. Add chicken livers to drippings in skillet; sprinkle lightly with salt. Cook and stir till lightly browned on all sides. Add beans, celery, soup, pimiento, Parmesan cheese, and ¼ cup water; mix lightly. Cover and cook over medium-low heat for 10 minutes. Garnish with crumbled bacon. Serves 6.

Baked Liver and Rice

1 cup long grain rice
3 cups milk
¼ cup chopped onion
1 tablespoon margarine or butter
1½ pounds beef liver, ground (2½ cups)
¼ pound ground pork
½ cup raisins
3 tablespoons dark corn syrup
1½ teaspoons dried marjoram, crushed

In saucepan combine uncooked rice and 2 cups water; bring to boiling, stirring once or twice. Simmer, uncovered, till water is absorbed, about 10 minutes. Add milk; cook over low heat, stirring occasionally, till the rice is tender, 10 to 15 minutes. Meanwhile, cook chopped onion in margarine or butter till tender but not brown.

  In bowl combine cooked rice, onion, ground liver, ground pork, raisins, corn syrup, marjoram, 2 teaspoons salt, and dash pepper. Spread meat mixture into a well-greased 13x9x2-inch baking dish. Bake at 400° for 40 to 45 minutes. Serves 12.

Liver-Tomato Supreme

2 slices bacon
1 pound beef liver, cut in
    ¼-inch strips
¼ cup all-purpose flour
½ cup chopped onion
½ cup chopped green pepper
1 16-ounce can tomatoes, cut up
½ teaspoon curry powder
Hot cooked rice

In skillet cook bacon till crisp; drain, reserving drippings. Crumble bacon and set aside. Coat liver with flour, and brown in reserved drippings; remove from skillet. In same skillet cook onion and green pepper till vegetables are tender. (Add cooking oil, if necessary.) Add undrained tomatoes, curry powder, ¼ cup water, 1 teaspoon salt, and ⅛ teaspoon pepper. Cover; simmer 25 to 30 minutes. Add liver; heat through. Serve liver over rice; top with bacon. Serves 5.

Chinese-Style Liver

⅓ cup sliced green onion with tops
2 tablespoons dry sherry
2 teaspoons cornstarch
¼ teaspoon ground ginger
1 pound beef liver, cut in
    ¼-inch strips
2 tablespoons cooking oil
1 5- or 6-ounce can bamboo shoots,
    drained
1 3-ounce can chopped mushrooms,
    drained
1 tablespoon soy sauce
Hot cooked rice
Soy sauce

Combine onion, sherry, cornstarch, and ginger; toss with liver. In skillet quickly cook liver in hot oil. Add bamboo shoots and mushrooms. Cook, stirring constantly, till heated through. Stir in 1 tablespoon soy sauce. Serve over rice. Pass soy sauce. Serves 4.

Tongue with Vegetable Gravy

1 2- to 3-pound fresh beef tongue
4 bay leaves
1 teaspoon whole peppercorns
1 teaspoon dried thyme, crushed
1 medium potato, peeled and diced
1 medium onion, chopped
1 medium tomato, cut up
½ cup chopped celery
½ cup chopped carrot
3 tablespoons all-purpose flour
  Hot cooked noodles

In Dutch oven cover tongue with water. Tie bay leaves, peppercorns, and thyme in cheesecloth bag; add with 1½ teaspoons salt to tongue. Cover and simmer till tongue is tender, about 2 hours. Add vegetables and cook about 30 minutes longer. Remove meat; drain. Cut off bones and gristle from large end. Split skin on underside from large end to tip; peel off. Slice tongue on a slant; keep warm while preparing vegetables.

Remove cheesecloth bag. Drain vegetables, reserving 2 cups liquid. Return vegetables and reserved liquid to Dutch oven. Blend ¼ cup cold water into flour; stir into mixture in Dutch oven. Cook and stir till thickened and bubbly. Season to taste. Serve tongue and vegetables with noodles. Serves 6 to 8.

Cheesy Tongue on Rice

2 cups shredded sharp American cheese
½ teaspoon dry mustard
¾ cup milk
½ teaspoon Worcestershire sauce
  Dash cayenne
1 beaten egg
1½ cups cooked tongue cut in thin
      strips 3 inches long
  Hot cooked rice

In saucepan toss cheese with mustard. Add milk. Stir over low heat till cheese melts and mixture is smooth. Stir in Worcestershire and cayenne. Stir moderate amount of hot mixture into egg. Return to hot mixture. Stir in tongue. Cook and stir till mixture is thick and creamy. Serve over rice. Serves 4.

Tongue-Green Bean Casserole

2 tablespoons chopped green onion
2 tablespoons margarine or butter
3 tablespoons all-purpose flour
1 teaspoon prepared mustard
¾ teaspoon Worcestershire sauce
¼ teaspoon salt
1 8-ounce can tomatoes, cut up
1 cup milk
2 cups cubed cooked tongue
1 16-ounce can cut green beans, drained
¾ cup soft bread crumbs
1 tablespoon margarine, melted

In saucepan cook onion in 2 tablespoons margarine till tender but not brown. Blend in flour, mustard, Worcestershire sauce, salt, and dash pepper. Add undrained tomatoes and milk. Cook and stir till thickened and bubbly. Remove from heat; stir in tongue and green beans. Turn into a 1½-quart casserole. Combine bread crumbs and 1 tablespoon margarine; sprinkle atop casserole. Bake at 350° for 30 minutes. Makes 4 servings.

Marinated Beef Heart Slices

1 2-pound beef heart
¼ cup finely chopped onion
¼ cup vinegar
¼ cup water
2 tablespoons cooking oil
1 bay leaf
½ teaspoon salt
¼ teaspoon pepper
⅛ teaspoon ground cloves
  Few drops bottled hot pepper sauce
1 carrot, finely chopped

Trim beef heart, removing skin, fat, and hard parts. Cut into ¼-inch-thick slices. Place meat slices in plastic bag in a deep bowl. Add next 9 ingredients. Close plastic bag and shake a few times to combine marinade. Refrigerate several hours. Drain heart and onions, reserving 2 tablespoons of the marinade. In an 8-inch skillet combine heart, onion, the 2 tablespoons of marinade, carrot, and ¼ cup water; simmer, cover, till meat is fork tender, about 45 minutes. Serves 4.

Kidney-Vegetable Dinner

2 pounds beef kidney
1 16-ounce can tomatoes, cut up
1 10½-ounce can condensed beef broth
2 tablespoons sliced green onion
1 clove garlic, minced
1 16-ounce can cut green beans, drained
1 cup coarsely chopped carrot
2 tablespoons dry red wine
3 tablespoons all-purpose flour

• • •

Hot cooked noodles

Slit kidney lengthwise down center; remove membranes and hard parts. Cut meat into ½-inch pieces. In large saucepan combine kidney, undrained tomatoes, beef broth, onion, garlic, and ½ teaspoon salt. Bring to boiling; reduce heat. Cover and simmer 1½ hours. Add beans and carrot; continue cooking till tender, about 25 minutes longer. Slowly stir wine and 2 tablespoons cold water into flour till smooth. Stir into kidney mixture; cook and stir till thickened and bubbly. Serve over noodles. Makes 6 to 8 servings.

Tripe and Onions

1½ pounds beef honeycomb tripe
½ cup chopped onion
¼ cup margarine or butter
3 tablespoons all-purpose flour
Dash ground nutmeg
1 cup chicken broth
1 cup milk

• • •

Toast points
Paprika

In saucepan cover tripe with water. Bring to a boil. Reduce heat; cook, covered, till cut surface of tripe has clear, jellylike appearance, about 3 hours. Drain and dice tripe.

Cook onion in margarine till tender but not brown. Blend in flour, nutmeg, 1 teaspoon salt, and ⅛ teaspoon pepper. Add chicken broth and milk all at once. Cook and stir till mixture is thickened and bubbly. Add tripe; heat through. Serve over toast points. Sprinkle with paprika. Makes 4 servings.

Sweetbread Supper

1 pound beef sweetbreads
4 cups water
1 tablespoon vinegar
¼ cup finely chopped celery
2 tablespoons finely chopped onion
¼ cup margarine or butter
¼ cup all-purpose flour
1 cup chicken broth
1 cup milk
2 tablespoons chopped canned pimiento
2 teaspoons lemon juice
12 frozen waffles

Simmer the sweetbreads in water, vinegar, and ½ teaspoon salt till tender, about 20 minutes. Drain. Cube sweetbreads, removing the white membrane. Cook celery and onion in margarine till tender. Blend in flour and ¼ teaspoon salt. Add chicken broth and milk all at once. Cook and stir till thickened and bubbly. Stir in sweetbreads, pimiento, and lemon juice. Heat through. Meanwhile, heat frozen waffles according to the package directions for oven method. Serve sweetbread mixture over waffles. Makes 6 servings.

Scrambled Brains

¼ pound beef or pork brains
1½ teaspoons vinegar
2 tablespoons margarine or butter
4 beaten eggs
1 tablespoon milk

Cover brains with cold water; add vinegar. Soak 30 minutes; drain. Remove fatty membrane. Cover brains with water; add ½ teaspoon salt. Simmer 20 to 30 minutes. Drain; chill in cold water. Finely chop brains.

In skillet brown the brains in margarine. Combine eggs, milk, and ¼ teaspoon salt; add to brains. Turn heat low. Don't disturb mixture till it starts to set on bottom and sides, then lift and fold over with wide spatula so uncooked part goes to bottom. Avoid breaking up eggs any more than necessary. Continue cooking till eggs are cooked but still glossy and moist, 5 to 8 minutes. Remove from heat immediately. Makes 4 servings.

Easy Cassoulet

2 lamb shoulder chops
2 pork shoulder chops
1 medium onion, chopped
2 cloves garlic, minced
3 tablespoons cooking oil
1 beef bouillon cube
½ cup boiling water
2 15-ounce cans great northern beans,
    drained
2 tablespoons chili sauce
1 teaspoon salt
¼ teaspoon pepper
¼ teaspoon dried thyme, crushed
4 strips bacon, crisp-cooked,
    drained, and crumbled

Remove lamb and pork from bones; cut into bite-size pieces. Discard bones. In saucepan cook meat cubes, onion, and garlic in hot oil till meat is browned and onion is tender. Dissolve bouillon cube in boiling water. Add to meat mixture with beans, chili sauce, salt, pepper, and thyme. Turn into 2-quart casserole. Bake, uncovered, at 350° for 30 minutes. Stir mixture; sprinkle bacon over top and continue baking, uncovered, for 30 to 45 minutes more. Makes 6 servings.

Mandarin Lamb Shanks

6 lamb shanks
  Cooking oil
1 10½-ounce can condensed beef broth
1 cup long grain rice
1 11-ounce can mandarin orange sections

In skillet brown the lamb on all sides in a small amount of hot oil; season with salt and pepper. Add 1 cup water; cover and simmer for 1¼ hours. Remove shanks; set aside. Measure pan juices; skim off fat and add water to make 1 cup liquid. Return to skillet with broth, uncooked rice, and ½ teaspoon salt.

Return lamb shanks to skillet; cover and simmer till rice is almost tender, about 25 minutes more. Stir in undrained oranges; simmer 10 minutes. Arrange rice mixture and lamb shanks on warm serving platter. Serves 6.

Lamb Patties with Dill Sauce

1 beaten egg
½ cup milk
¾ cup quick-cooking rolled oats
¼ cup snipped parsley
¼ cup finely chopped onion
1½ pounds ground lamb
  Dill Sauce

Combine egg, milk, oats, parsley, onion, 1 teaspoon salt, and ⅛ teaspoon pepper. Add lamb; mix well. Form into eight 3-inch-thick patties. Broil 4 to 5 inches from heat, about 6 minutes. Turn patties; broil 5 to 6 minutes longer. Serve with Dill Sauce. Serves 8.

Dill Sauce: In saucepan combine one 10½-ounce can condensed cream of celery soup, ⅓ cup milk, and ½ teaspoon dried dillweed; heat through. Makes 1½ cups.

Ground Lamb Pizza

1 pound ground lamb *or* ground beef
½ cup chopped onion
1 teaspoon chili powder
1 teaspoon dried oregano, crushed
½ teaspoon dried basil, crushed
⅛ teaspoon pepper
1 package active dry yeast
2¾ cups Basic Biscuit Mix (see recipe,
    page 20)
  Cooking oil
2 8-ounce cans tomato sauce with cheese
2 cups shredded mozzarella cheese

Cook lamb and onion till meat is browned. Drain off fat. Add chili powder, oregano, basil, and pepper. Soften yeast in ¾ cup warm water (110°). Add Basic Biscuit Mix; blend thoroughly. Sprinkle surface lightly with flour; knead dough till smooth (25 strokes). Divide dough in half; cover and let rest 10 minutes. Roll out each half of the dough and fit into a greased 12-inch pizza pan. Crimp edges. Brush dough with cooking oil. Bake at 425° for 10 minutes. Pour *half* the tomato sauce over *each* pizza. Sprinkle *half* the meat mixture over *each* pizza. Top the pizzas with mozzarella cheese. Bake at 425° for 12 to 15 minutes. Makes 6 to 8 servings.

Mustard-Brushed Bologna Kabobs

¼ cup margarine or butter, melted
2 tablespoons Dijon-style mustard
1 tablespoon snipped parsley
2 teaspoons lemon juice
  Dash pepper
1 pound chunk bologna, cut into 1-inch
  cubes
1 13¼-ounce can pineapple chunks,
  drained

Combine margarine, mustard, parsley, lemon juice, and pepper. Thread bologna cubes on skewers alternately with pineapple chunks. Brush with mustard mixture. Grill over medium coals, turning frequently till heated through, 8 to 10 minutes. Brush often with the mustard mixture. Makes 4 servings.

Sausage-Noodle Skillet

1 pound bulk pork sausage
¼ cup chopped onion
• • •
2 cups medium noodles
1 10¾-ounce can condensed tomato soup
1¼ cups water
1 teaspoon Worcestershire sauce
2 tablespoons snipped parsley

In large skillet cook the sausage and onion till sausage is browned and the onion is tender; drain off excess fat. Add uncooked noodles, tomato soup, water, and the Worcestershire sauce; bring to boiling. Reduce heat and simmer sausage mixture, uncovered, 15 minutes, stirring occasionally. Stir in the snipped parsley. Makes 4 servings.

Making *Hawaiian Sausage Casserole* is a snap. Simply combine smoked sausage links and canned sweet potatoes, then for an interesting flavor contrast add pineapple chunks and brown sugar.

Hawaiian Sausage Casserole

    1 20-ounce can pineapple chunks
        (juice pack)
    1 17-ounce can sweet potatoes, sliced
        1 inch thick
    1 12-ounce package fully cooked smoked
        sausage links, slashed at 1-inch
        intervals
    3 tablespoons packed brown sugar
    2 tablespoons cornstarch
    ¼ teaspoon salt
    1 tablespoon margarine or butter

Drain the pineapple, reserving juice. Add water to juice to make 1¼ cups. Arrange pineapple, potatoes, and sausage in 10x6x2-inch baking dish. In saucepan combine brown sugar, cornstarch, and salt. Gradually blend in reserved juice. Cook and stir till thickened and bubbly; cook and stir 1 minute more. Remove from heat; stir in margarine. Pour sauce over casserole. Cover and bake at 350° till hot, 35 to 40 minutes. Serves 4 to 6.

Savory Sausage Skillet

    1 pound fresh pork sausage links, cut
        in thirds
    1 tablespoon chopped onion
    1 clove garlic, minced
    ¾ cup milk
    ⅓ cup Beef Gravy Base (see recipe,
        page 18)
    2 tablespoons catsup
    1 tablespoon snipped parsley
    1 teaspoon Dijon-style mustard
    ½ teaspoon Worcestershire sauce
        Seasoned Rice Mix (see
            recipe, page 21)

In skillet cook the sausage links till browned, 7 to 8 minutes, turning occasionally. Drain off excess fat. Add onion and garlic; cook the onion till tender but not brown. Combine next 6 ingredients and ⅔ cup water. Add to sausage in skillet and heat the mixture till thickened and bubbly.

Prepare Seasoned Rice Mix according to recipe directions. Serve sausage mixture over Seasoned Rice. Makes 4 to 6 servings.

Smoked Sausage Curry

    ⅔ cup long grain rice
    2 medium apples, cut in wedges and
        cored
    1 medium onion, cut in wedges
    2 tablespoons margarine or butter
    1 beef bouillon cube
    1 tablespoon cornstarch
    1½ teaspoons curry powder
    1 12-ounce package fully cooked smoked
        sausage links
    ½ cup raisins

Prepare rice according to package directions. In skillet brown the apples and onion in margarine; remove and set aside. In the same skillet dissolve bouillon cube in 1 cup hot water; bring to boiling. Combine cornstarch, curry powder, and ¼ cup cold water. Add to hot bouillon; cook and stir till mixture thickens. Add sausage, onion, and apples. Cook, uncovered, over low heat till apples and onion are tender, about 5 minutes.

Meanwhile cover raisins with water; bring to boiling. Remove from heat; let stand 5 minutes. Combine hot rice and raisins; place on platter. Remove sausage from sauce and arrange atop rice mixture. Pour sauce with apples and onion over all. Serves 4.

Sausage-Corn Bake

    8 ounces fresh pork sausage links
    1 17-ounce can cream-style corn
    1 cup milk
    1 beaten egg
    1 cup finely crushed saltine crackers
    2 tablespoons chopped onion
    2 tablespoons finely chopped green
        pepper
    ¾ teaspoon salt
    ⅛ teaspoon pepper

Cook sausages till browned, 7 to 8 minutes, turning occasionally. Drain. Heat corn and milk together. Stir in remaining ingredients *except sausages.* Turn into an 8x1½-inch round baking dish; top with sausages. Bake at 350° till knife inserted off-center comes out clean, 25 to 30 minutes. Serves 4.

Sausage Meatball Fondue

Cook ½ pound bulk pork sausage, finely crumbled, and ¼ cup finely chopped onion till meat is browned; drain. Add one 16-ounce can sauerkraut, well drained and snipped, and 2 tablespoons fine dry bread crumbs. Combine one 3-ounce package cream cheese, softened; 2 tablespoons snipped parsley; 1 teaspoon prepared mustard; ¼ teaspoon garlic salt; and ⅛ teaspoon pepper. Stir into meat.

Chill meat mixture. Shape into ¾-inch balls; coat with ¼ cup all-purpose flour. Combine 2 beaten eggs and ¼ cup milk. Roll balls in egg mixture, then in ¾ cup fine dry bread crumbs. Pour cooking oil into metal fondue cooker to no more than half capacity or to a depth of 2 inches. Heat over range to 375°. Transfer to fondue burner. Have meatballs at room temperature. Spear with fondue fork; fry in hot oil till golden, 30 to 60 seconds. Transfer to dinner fork; dip in Mustard Sauce or Quick Curry Dip. Serves 4.

Mustard Sauce: Stir together ½ cup salad dressing or mayonnaise and 2 tablespoons prepared mustard. Makes ½ cup sauce.

Quick Curry Dip: Combine ½ cup dairy sour cream and ½ teaspoon curry powder. Chill thoroughly. Makes ½ cup sauce.

Scalloped Sausage and Potatoes

   1 pound bulk pork sausage
   4 cups thinly sliced potatoes
   ¼ cup all-purpose flour
   ¼ teaspoon salt
   1 cup shredded sharp American
      cheese (4 ounces)
   1½ cups milk

In skillet crumble sausage and brown it lightly; drain thoroughly. Place *half* of the sliced potatoes in a 2-quart casserole. Combine flour and salt. Sprinkle *half* the seasoned flour mixture over the potatoes. Top with *half* the browned sausage and *half* of the cheese. Repeat layers with remaining potatoes, flour mixture, sausage, and cheese. Pour milk over all. Cover and bake at 350° till potatoes are tender, 50 to 60 minutes. Uncover and bake 10 minutes more. Makes 4 to 6 servings.

Hot Luncheon Meat Casserole

   4 ounces medium noodles
   ½ cup chopped onion
   1 tablespoon margarine or butter
   1 12-ounce can luncheon meat
   1 16-ounce can tomatoes, cut up
   1 15½-ounce can red kidney beans,
      drained
   ½ teaspoon dry mustard
   ½ teaspoon dried marjoram, crushed
   ¼ teaspoon dried basil, crushed
   6 to 8 drops bottled hot pepper sauce
   ½ cup shredded sharp American
      cheese (2 ounces)

Cook noodles in boiling salted water till almost tender; drain. In saucepan cook onion in margarine till tender. Cut luncheon meat into ½-inch cubes and add to onion. Stir in next 6 ingredients; bring mixture to boiling. Stir in noodles. Turn mixture into a 2-quart casserole. Bake at 375° for 25 minutes. Stir; top with cheese and return to oven till cheese melts, about 5 minutes. Serves 6.

Stuffed Baked Potatoes

This tasty dish is shown on page 22 —

   4 large baking potatoes
   ½ cup margarine or butter, softened
   ½ teaspoon garlic salt
   ½ teaspoon dried basil, crushed
   ½ teaspoon dried oregano, crushed
   1 12-ounce can luncheon meat
   4 slices American cheese, cut in
      half diagonally
   2 teaspoons grated Parmesan cheese

Bake potatoes at 425° for 45 minutes. Blend together margarine and seasonings; set aside. Slice each potato crosswise into 4 pieces. Cut meat in half crosswise, then cut each half into 6 slices crosswise. Insert a slice of meat between potato pieces. Reassemble potato and wrap in foil, but do not close top. (Or, hold potato together with skewer.) Bake at 350° for 10 minutes. Place cheese triangles on top; bake till cheese melts, about 1 minute. Sprinkle with Parmesan. Serve with margarine mixture. Serves 4.

Peachy Luncheon Meat

Try this dish when you need a meal in a hurry—

1 12-ounce can luncheon meat, cut into
   slices
1 16-ounce can peach slices

In a medium skillet brown the luncheon meat slices on both sides. Push slices to one side of skillet. Drain peach slices, reserving ¼ cup syrup. Place peach slices in skillet; spoon reserved syrup over luncheon meat and fruit. Cook till heated through, about 5 minutes. Makes 4 servings.

Luncheon Meat-Cheese Bake

1 10-ounce package frozen chopped
   broccoli
8 slices white bread
1 cup shredded sharp American
   cheese (4 ounces)
1 12-ounce can luncheon meat, cut in
   strips

• • •

5 beaten eggs
3 cups milk
2 tablespoons finely chopped onion
1 teaspoon Worcestershire sauce

In a saucepan cook the broccoli according to package directions; drain well. Trim the crusts from *6 slices* of the bread; cut trimmed pieces in half diagonally. Use bread trimmings and the remaining 2 slices untrimmed bread to cover the bottom of a greased 12x7½x2-inch baking dish. Top with cheese, drained broccoli, and luncheon meat strips. Arrange the 12 trimmed bread triangles on top in two rows. Points of bread triangles should overlap bases of previous triangles.

In a large bowl combine beaten eggs, milk, chopped onion, and the Worcestershire sauce. Pour the egg mixture over the bread triangles. Let stand about 30 minutes. Bake casserole at 350° till a knife inserted halfway between center and edge comes out clean, about 50 minutes. (If bread browns excessively, cover baking dish with foil during last 15 minutes.) Let the casserole stand 5 minutes before serving. Makes 6 to 8 servings.

Fruited Meat Pie

½ cup finely chopped onion
½ cup finely chopped celery
1 17-ounce can fruit cocktail
2 tablespoons cornstarch
2 tablespoons packed brown sugar
¾ teaspoon dry mustard
   Dash ground cloves
1 12-ounce can luncheon meat,
   cut in ½-inch strips
3 tablespoons lemon juice
   Pastry for a 1-crust 9-inch pie (see
   recipe, page 17)

Cook onion and celery, covered, in a small amount of boiling water till just tender, 3 to 5 minutes; drain. Drain fruit cocktail, reserving syrup. Combine cornstarch, brown sugar, mustard, and cloves; stir in reserved syrup. Cook and stir till thickened and bubbly. Stir in fruit cocktail, luncheon meat, onion, celery, and lemon juice. Pour into an 8x1½-inch round baking dish. Roll pastry to a 9-inch circle. Place pastry atop meat mixture; turn under and crimp edges. Bake at 425° for 20 to 25 minutes. Makes 4 to 6 servings.

Luncheon Meat-Rice Supper

⅔ cup long grain rice
⅓ cup finely chopped onion
1 10-ounce package frozen peas
1 12-ounce can luncheon meat
1 10½-ounce can condensed cream of
   chicken soup
1 cup milk
¼ cup snipped parsley
½ teaspoon poultry seasoning

In saucepan combine uncooked rice, onion, 1⅓ cups water, and ½ teaspoon salt. Bring to boiling; reduce heat and simmer for 14 minutes. Remove from heat; let stand, covered, 10 minutes. Cook peas according to package directions; drain. Cut luncheon meat into ½-inch cubes. Combine with rice mixture and peas. Mix remaining ingredients and dash pepper together. Stir into rice mixture. Spread in 10x6x2-inch baking dish. Cover and bake at 350° for 35 to 40 minutes. Serves 6.

Sweet and Sour Franks

½ cup chopped onion
1 medium green pepper, cut in 1-inch
 strips
2 tablespoons margarine or butter,
 melted
1 8½-ounce can pineapple tidbits
1 teaspoon instant beef bouillon
 granules
1 cup boiling water
2 tablespoons cornstarch
1 tablespoon packed brown sugar
 Dash salt
2 tablespoons vinegar
1 tablespoon soy sauce
4 or 5 frankfurters, cut in 1-inch
 pieces (8 ounces)
• • •
 Hot cooked rice

In a medium skillet cook chopped onion and green pepper in margarine or butter till vegetables are tender, but not brown. Drain pineapple tidbits, reserving syrup. Dissolve bouillon granules in boiling water. Mix corn-starch, brown sugar, and salt. Blend in reserved pineapple syrup, bouillon, vinegar, and soy sauce. Pour over vegetables. Cook and stir till thickened and bubbly. Add franks and pineapple tidbits. Heat through. Serve over cooked rice. Makes 4 servings.

Franks with Apple Kraut

4 tart apples, peeled, cored, and
 sliced
1 27-ounce can sauerkraut
¼ cup packed brown sugar
1 teaspoon caraway seed
• • •
8 or 10 frankfurters, cut diagonally
 in 1-inch pieces (1 pound)

In large saucepan combine the apple slices, undrained sauerkraut, brown sugar, and the caraway seed. Bring apple mixture to boiling; reduce heat and simmer, covered, 20 minutes. Stir in the frankfurter pieces and simmer the mixture till heated through, about 10 minutes more. Makes 6 servings.

Frank-Potato Pie

4 or 5 frankfurters, cut in 1-inch
 pieces (8 ounces)
½ cup chopped onion
2 tablespoons margarine or butter,
 melted
1 16-ounce can cut green beans, drained
1 10¾-ounce can condensed tomato soup
 Packaged instant mashed potatoes
 (enough for 4 servings)
1 beaten egg
½ cup shredded sharp American cheese
 (2 ounces)

Cook frankfurters and onion in margarine till franks are browned and onion is tender. Stir in green beans and tomato soup. Turn into a 1½-quart casserole. Set aside.

Prepare mashed potatoes according to package directions, *except reserve the milk.* Add beaten egg. Slowly add enough of the reserved milk to make potatoes hold shape. Mound potatoes on top of frankfurter mixture. Bake, uncovered, at 350° for 25 minutes; top with cheese. Bake till cheese is melted, about 5 minutes. Serves 6.

Frankfurter-Bean Bake

1 cup dry navy beans (8 ounces)
4 cups water
½ cup chopped onion
¼ cup packed brown sugar
¼ cup molasses
½ teaspoon dry mustard
4 or 5 frankfurters, cut in 1-inch
 pieces (8 ounces)

Rinse navy beans. In large saucepan cover beans with the water. Bring to boiling; simmer 2 minutes. Remove from heat; cover and let stand 1 hour. Cover pan; simmer till tender, 1 hour. Drain beans, reserving ½ cup liquid. Stir together beans, reserved liquid, onion, brown sugar, molasses, mustard, and ¼ teaspoon salt. Turn into a 2-quart casserole. Cover and bake at 350° for 1 hour. Add frankfurters and bake, covered, till heated through, 15 minutes more. Stir before serving. Serves 4 to 6.

Hungarian Frank Bake

 4 ounces medium noodles
 2 tablespoons cooking oil
 1 tablespoon sugar
 1¾ teaspoons salt
 8 cups chopped cabbage
 1 cup milk
 2 tablespoons all-purpose flour
 1 cup dairy sour cream
 8 or 10 frankfurters, cut crosswise
    in fourths (1 pound)
    Paprika

Cook noodles in boiling salted water till tender; drain. In large skillet combine oil, sugar, and salt. Add the cabbage; stir till cabbage is coated. Cook, covered, over medium-low heat till cabbage is tender, about 10 minutes. In saucepan stir milk into flour; cook and stir till thickened and bubbly. Stir in sour cream. Combine cabbage, noodles, sour cream mixture, and frankfurters. Turn into a 2-quart casserole. Bake, covered, at 350° for 30 to 35 minutes. Sprinkle the top with paprika. Makes 8 servings.

Quick Frank Kabobs

 8 frankfurters
 1 16-ounce can whole new potatoes,
    drained
 2 medium green peppers, cut in pieces
    • • •
 ¼ cup horseradish mustard
 ¼ cup catsup
 ½ envelope taco seasoning mix
    (about 2 tablespoons)
 2 tablespoons water
 2 tablespoons cooking oil
    Several drops bottled hot pepper
    sauce

Cut the frankfurters into thirds. Place on skewers alternately with potatoes and green pepper pieces. In small bowl stir together horseradish mustard, catsup, seasoning mix, water, oil, and the hot pepper sauce.

 Grill the kabobs over medium coals for 10 minutes, turning often and brushing with mustard mixture. Makes 4 to 6 servings.

Jiffy Frankfurter Supper

 1 8½-ounce can pineapple tidbits
 1 cup White Sauce Mix (see recipe,
    page 19)
 1 small green pepper, cut in strips
 1 tablespoon soy sauce
 1 beaten egg
 6 frankfurters, sliced
 1 3-ounce can chow mein noodles

Drain the pineapple, reserving syrup; add water to syrup to make 2 cups liquid. In saucepan combine the White Sauce Mix, reserved pineapple syrup mixture, green pepper strips, and the soy sauce. Cook and stir till thickened and bubbly. Stir a moderate amount of hot mixture into the beaten egg. Return to saucepan. Cook, stirring constantly, about 1 minute. Stir in sliced frankfurters and the drained pineapple. Heat the mixture through. Serve over the chow mein noodles. Serves 6.

Mexican-Style Franks

 1 11-ounce can condensed chili beef
    soup
 ½ cup chopped onion
 ⅓ cup water
 ¼ cup chopped green pepper
    Dash bottled hot pepper sauce
 4 frankfurters, cut in half lengthwise
 8 canned tortillas or frozen tortillas,
    thawed
 1 8-ounce can tomato sauce
 ¼ cup water
    • • •
 ½ cup shredded American cheese
    (2 ounces)

Combine the chili beef soup, onion, ⅓ cup water, green pepper, and the bottled hot pepper sauce. Place a frankfurter half on each tortilla; top each with *1 tablespoon* of the chili soup mixture. Roll the tortillas around frankfurters. Arrange the tortillas, seam side down, in 10x6x2-inch baking dish.

 Combine the remaining chili soup mixture, tomato sauce, and ¼ cup water; pour over tortillas. Bake at 350° for 30 minutes. Top with shredded cheese and serve hot. Serves 4.

Sandwiches and main dish salads

Sauerbraten Burgers

Combine 1 beaten egg, ½ cup chopped onion, ⅓ cup milk, ¼ cup fine dry bread crumbs, and 1 teaspoon salt. Add 1½ pounds ground beef; mix well. Shape into 6 patties. In skillet brown the patties on both sides; drain fat. Add 1½ cups water, ½ cup coarsely crushed gingersnaps, ⅓ cup packed brown sugar, ¼ cup raisins, 3 tablespoons lemon juice, and 2 beef bouillon cubes. Bring to boiling. Cover; simmer 30 minutes, stirring often. Serve with hot cooked noodles. Serves 6.

Cheese-Stuffed Burgers

　¾ cup White Sauce Mix (see recipe,
　　　page 19)
1¼ cups milk
1½ cups shredded sharp American
　　　cheese (6 ounces)
　1 beaten egg
　1 cup soft bread crumbs
　1 pound ground beef
　1 3-ounce can chopped mushrooms
　½ cup cooked rice
　1 tablespoon chopped green onion

Blend White Sauce Mix into milk; cook and stir till thickened. Stir in cheese till melted. Combine egg, ⅓ *cup* of the cheese sauce, and crumbs; mix in meat. Shape into four 6-inch patties. Drain mushrooms. Combine ¼ *cup* of the mushrooms, rice, and onion. Spoon 2 tablespoons mixture onto each patty. Seal meat around stuffing. Bake, uncovered, in 8x8x2-inch baking pan at 350° for 45 minutes. Combine remaining sauce and mushrooms; heat. Serve over burgers. Serves 4.

Delectable beefburgers

← Beer is the perfect beverage to go with *Cheese-Stuffed Burgers.* Serve this different burger version with a cheese sauce and trim with red peppers and sprigs of parsley, if desired.

Sproutburgers

　½ cup chopped onion
　1 tablespoon cooking oil
　1 beaten egg
　1 cup whole wheat bread crumbs
　⅔ cup canned bean sprouts
　¼ cup catsup
　¾ teaspoon salt
　½ teaspoon dry mustard
　⅛ teaspoon pepper
　1 pound ground beef
　½ cup wheat germ
　　Cooking oil

Cook onion in 1 tablespoon oil till tender. Combine onion and next 7 ingredients. Add meat; mix well. Form into 6 patties; coat with wheat germ. In skillet fry patties in small amount of hot oil; turn once. Serves 6.

Giant Stuffed Grillburger

　1 beaten egg
1¼ cups herb-seasoned stuffing
　　　mix, crushed (¾ cup)
　1 3-ounce can chopped mushrooms,
　　　drained
　⅓ cup beef broth
　¼ cup sliced green onion
　¼ cup snipped parsley
　2 tablespoons margarine, melted
　1 teaspoon lemon juice
　2 pounds ground beef

Mix together first 8 ingredients; set aside. Combine meat and 1 teaspoon salt; divide in half. On sheets of waxed paper, pat each half to an 8-inch circle. Spoon stuffing over one circle of meat to within 1 inch of edge. Top with second circle of meat; peel off top sheet of paper and seal edges. Invert meat patty onto a well-greased grill basket; peel off remaining paper. Grill over medium coals till done, 10 to 12 minutes on each side. Cut into wedges; serve with warmed catsup, if desired. Makes 8 servings.

Smoked Beef and Bean Burgers

    1 8-ounce can red kidney beans,
        drained
    1 3½-ounce package sliced smoked
        beef, snipped
    ⅓ cup salad dressing or mayonnaise
    2 tablespoons finely chopped onion
    2 tablespoons sweet pickle relish
    1½ teaspoons prepared mustard
    6 hamburger buns, split and toasted
            • • •
    3 slices American cheese,
        halved (3 ounces)

In a bowl slightly mash the drained kidney beans. Add the snipped beef, salad dressing or mayonnaise, chopped onion, sweet pickle relish, and mustard; mix thoroughly. Spread bean mixture on bottom halves of the hamburger buns. Broil 5 inches from heat for 3 minutes. Top each sandwich with ½ slice of cheese and the top halves of the hamburger buns. Return the sandwiches to the broiler to melt cheese and to toast the buns. Serve the sandwiches hot. Makes 6 sandwiches.

Frankwiches

Serve this tasty combo of frankfurters and tomato soup warm and toasty—

    8 or 10 frankfurters, chopped
        (1 pound)
    1 10¾-ounce can condensed tomato soup
    1 cup shredded sharp American cheese
        (4 ounces)
    ¼ cup chopped onion
    ¼ cup sweet pickle relish
    1 tablespoon prepared mustard
    1 teaspoon Worcestershire sauce
    12 hamburger buns, split and toasted

In medium bowl combine the chopped frankfurters, tomato soup, shredded cheese, onion, sweet pickle relish, prepared mustard, and Worcestershire sauce. Thoroughly mix the ingredients. Spoon about ⅓ *cup* of the filling onto each toasted hamburger bun. Wrap each sandwich in foil. Place the sandwiches on a baking sheet. Heat the sandwiches at 400° for 15 minutes. Makes 12 sandwiches.

Hobo-Logna Bunwiches

    8 ounces chunk bologna, cut in
        1x1x½-inch pieces
    1 13¼-ounce can pineapple chunks,
        drained
    2 green peppers, cut in 1-inch squares
            • • •
    ½ cup catsup
    2 tablespoons finely chopped onion
    2 tablespoons cooking oil
    1 tablespoon lemon juice
    1 teaspoon dry mustard
    8 frankfurter buns, split and toasted
        Margarine or butter

On skewers alternately thread pieces of bologna, pineapple, and green pepper. Combine the catsup, onion, cooking oil, lemon juice, and mustard. Broil the kabobs over slow coals 5 minutes; brush with the catsup mixture. Broil the kabobs 10 minutes more, brushing with the sauce and turning frequently. Spread the frankfurter buns with margarine. Serve the hot kabobs on buns. Makes 8 sandwiches.

Bologna-Cheese Club Sandwiches

    6 ounces chunk bologna
    4 slices pimiento cheese
        (4 ounces)
    ¼ small onion
    3 small sweet pickles
    3 tablespoons salad dressing or
        mayonnaise
    2 tablespoons chopped green pepper
    2 teaspoons prepared mustard
    18 slices sandwich-style rye bread
        Margarine or butter
        Lettuce
    2 tomatoes, sliced

Grind together bologna, pimiento cheese, onion, and pickles. Add salad dressing, green pepper, and mustard. Spread bread slices with margarine. Spread each of *6 slices* of rye bread with ¼ *cup* filling; top with *6 slices* bread. Arrange lettuce and sliced tomatoes atop. Cover sandwiches with remaining 6 slices of bread, buttered side down. Makes 6.

Bean Sprout-Chicken Sandwiches

Bean sprouts are a tasty change on sandwiches. Here they are used as a substitute for lettuce—

> 1 cup finely chopped cooked chicken
> ½ cup chopped celery
> 2 tablespoons snipped parsley
> ¼ cup salad dressing or mayonnaise
> 2 teaspoons soy sauce
> • • •
> Margarine or butter, softened
> 8 slices whole wheat bread
> 1 cup canned, drained bean sprouts

Combine chopped chicken, celery, and the snipped parsley. Blend together salad dressing or mayonnaise and soy sauce; add to the chicken mixture and stir lightly.

Spread the softened margarine or butter on one side of whole wheat bread slices. Spread the sandwich filling on the buttered side of *4 slices* bread. Top each with ¼ cup bean sprouts. Top with the remaining bread, buttered side down. Makes 4 sandwiches.

Braunschweiger Sandwiches

A delicious meal-in-one sandwich—

> 3 tablespoons salad dressing or
>   mayonnaise
> 3 tablespoons Dijon-style mustard
> • • •
> 10 slices dark rye *or* pumpernickel
>   bread, toasted
> 10 slices braunschweiger
> 5 slices Swiss cheese, halved
>   diagonally (5 ounces)
> 1 8-ounce can sauerkraut, heated and
>   drained

In a small bowl combine the salad dressing or mayonnaise and mustard. Spread the mixture on one side of each piece of the rye or pumpernickel toast. Top *half the slices* of toast with 2 slices braunschweiger and 2 half-slices Swiss cheese.

Broil sandwiches 4 to 5 inches from heat till heated through and the Swiss cheese has melted. Top each sandwich with ½ cup sauerkraut and the second piece of toast, dressing side down. Makes 5 sandwiches.

Denverwiches

> 6 hamburger buns, split
>   and toasted
> 1 4½-ounce can corned
>   beef spread
> 4 eggs
> ¼ cup water
> 1 tablespoon nonfat dry milk powder
> ¼ teaspoon salt
>   Dash pepper
> • • •
> ¼ cup chopped onion
> 2 tablespoons margarine or butter

Spread the bottom halves of toasted hamburger buns with the corned beef spread; set aside. Combine the eggs, water, milk powder, salt, and pepper. Thoroughly beat the ingredients together with a fork.

In a medium skillet cook chopped onion in margarine or butter till tender but not brown. Pour in egg mixture. Cook and stir till desired doneness. Pile the egg mixture atop the corned beef spread. Cover sandwiches with bun tops. Makes 6 servings.

Big Western Bean Burgers

A saucy sandwich that enhances the protein from beef with the protein from baked beans—

> ½ cup water
> 2 tablespoons onion soup mix
> • • •
> 1 18-ounce jar baked beans in
>   molasses sauce
> 1 3½-ounce package sliced smoked
>   beef, snipped
> 3 tablespoons sweet pickle relish
> 8 hamburger buns, split and toasted

In a medium saucepan combine water and the onion soup mix; let the mixture stand till softened, about 5 minutes.

In same saucepan stir in the baked beans in molasses sauce, snipped smoked beef, and the sweet pickle relish. Cook the sandwich filling over medium heat till the mixture is heated through, stirring occasionally. Spoon the hot sandwich filling into the toasted hamburger buns. Makes 8 sandwiches.

Ravioli Roulade

Unroll 1 package refrigerated crescent rolls (8 rolls). Separate rolls into 8 triangles. Set aside. Combine one 7½-ounce can chopped spinach, well drained; 1 cup finely diced fully cooked ham; and ⅓ cup shredded Monterey Jack cheese. Mix thoroughly. On each triangle place 2 tablespoons of the sandwich filling at wide end of triangle. Roll up, starting at the wide end.

Arrange the rolls, point side down, on greased baking sheet. Brush the rolls with 1 tablespoon milk. Bake the sandwiches at 375° for 20 to 25 minutes.

Meanwhile, combine 1 cup Marinara Sauce (see recipe, page 15) and 1 teaspoon dried oregano, crushed. Heat sauce through. Spoon over the sandwiches. Makes 4 servings.

Ham-Apple Burgers

2½ cups chopped fully cooked ham
½ cup chopped celery
2 tablespoons chopped onion
2 tablespoons margarine or butter
1½ cups chopped tart apple
½ cup dairy sour cream
¼ cup salad dressing or mayonnaise
1 teaspoon prepared horseradish
8 hamburger buns, split and toasted

In saucepan cook ham, celery, and onion in margarine or butter till vegetables are tender but not brown, 6 to 8 minutes. Stir chopped apple, sour cream, salad dressing or mayonnaise, and horseradish into ham mixture; heat through over low heat. Spoon the hot mixture into buns. Makes 8 sandwiches.

Ravioli Roulade features crescent rolls wrapped around a ham and spinach filling. The sandwiches are baked and topped with *Marinara Sauce* (see recipe, page 15). Garnish with pimiento-stuffed olives.

Sombrero Surprises

¾ pound ground beef
1 teaspoon salt
  Dash pepper
1 package refrigerated
    biscuits (10 biscuits)
  Catsup
  Prepared mustard
5 very thin slices onion
½ cup torn or shredded lettuce
5 slices American cheese
    (5 ounces)

Combine ground beef, salt, and pepper. Shape into 5 patties about 3 inches in diameter. In skillet brown the patties on both sides; drain off fat. On lightly floured board roll each refrigerated biscuit to a 5-inch circle. Spread *half* the circles with catsup and mustard; place beef patty atop each. Top with onion slice, then lettuce. Cover with remaining circles of dough. Moisten edges; press together with a fork to seal. Prick tops of each sandwich about 3 times with fork. Place on ungreased baking sheet. Bake at 375° for 10 to 12 minutes. Place a cheese slice atop each; return to oven till cheese melts, 2 to 3 minutes longer. Makes 5 servings.

Zesty Luncheon Barbecue

¼ cup chopped onion
1 tablespoon cooking oil
½ cup catsup
2 tablespoons packed brown sugar
1 tablespoon vinegar
1½ teaspoons Worcestershire sauce
1½ teaspoons prepared mustard
1 12-ounce can luncheon meat
4 slices French bread, toasted

In small saucepan cook onion in cooking oil till tender but not brown. Stir in catsup, brown sugar, vinegar, Worcestershire, and mustard; heat through. Cut luncheon meat into 8 slices. Place meat on grill; brush with sauce. Grill over medium-hot coals for 5 to 6 minutes on each side, brushing often with sauce. Serve 2 meat slices on each slice of French bread. Makes 4 open-face sandwiches.

Hot Corned Beef Sandwiches

1 12-ounce can corned beef, flaked
1 cup diced sharp American cheese
    (4 ounces)
½ cup salad dressing or mayonnaise
2 tablespoons sweet pickle relish
1 tablespoon instant minced onion
8 onion rolls *or* hamburger buns, split
  Margarine or butter

Mix together the corned beef, cheese, salad dressing, sweet pickle relish, and onion. Spread the onion rolls or hamburger buns with margarine or butter. Spoon the sandwich filling into the rolls. Wrap the sandwiches in heavy foil. Grill over medium-hot coals for 12 to 15 minutes, turning sandwiches several times, or bake at 375° till hot through, about 20 minutes. Makes 8 sandwiches.

Corned Beef Barbecue

In saucepan cook ¼ cup chopped onion and 2 tablespoons chopped green pepper in 2 tablespoons hot cooking oil till tender. Stir in one 12-ounce can corned beef, flaked, and ¾ cup chili sauce. Cook, stirring occasionally, till heated through, about 5 minutes. Serve in 6 to 8 hamburger buns, split and toasted. Makes 6 to 8 sandwiches.

Peanut Butter-Bacon Sandwiches

½ cup peanut butter
6 slices bacon, crisp cooked, drained,
    and crumbled
⅓ cup finely chopped celery
10 slices pumpernickel *or* white bread,
    toasted
  Margarine or butter
  Lettuce

Combine peanut butter, bacon, and celery. Spread the toast slices with margarine or butter. Spread *5 slices* of the toast with peanut butter mixture, using about 3 tablespoons mixture for each slice. Top the filling with lettuce and remaining toast slices, buttered side down. Makes 5 sandwiches.

Corned Beef-Potato Salad

⅔ cup salad dressing or mayonnaise
2 tablespoons milk
2 tablespoons prepared mustard
1 tablespoon vinegar
1 teaspoon sugar
½ teaspoon salt
2 medium potatoes
1½ cups finely shredded cabbage
1 12-ounce can corned beef, chilled
   and cubed

Combine salad dressing or mayonnaise, milk, mustard, vinegar, sugar, and salt; set aside. Meanwhile, cook potatoes in enough boiling salted water to cover, 20 to 30 minutes. Drain, peel, and cube potatoes. While the potatoes are warm, add salad dressing mixture; toss to coat. Chill. To serve, add cabbage and corned beef to mixture; toss. Makes 6 servings.

Marinated Vegetable-Beef Salad

1 9-ounce package frozen cut green
   beans, cooked and drained
1 cup sliced cucumber
1 cup cooked carrot strips
½ cup French salad dressing
6 cups torn lettuce
1 cup cooked beef cut in thin strips
3 hard-cooked eggs, sliced
½ cup salad dressing or mayonnaise
2 tablespoons chopped sweet pickle
1½ teaspoons prepared mustard
1 teaspoon prepared horseradish

Marinate beans, cucumber, and carrots in French dressing for 2 hours. Place lettuce in salad bowl. Arrange beef, eggs, and vegetables with marinade on top. Combine salad dressing, pickle, mustard, and horseradish; spoon over salad. Toss. Makes 6 servings.

A flavor-packed main dish salad

← Combine potatoes, corned beef, and shredded cabbage all into one dish by preparing *Corned Beef-Potato Salad*. Serve it with pieces of rye bread and glasses of cold beer.

Tostada Platter

1 pound ground beef
½ cup chopped onion
1 clove garlic, minced
½ teaspoon chili powder
1 8-ounce can cut green beans
1 8-ounce can red kidney beans
6 canned tortillas or frozen tortillas,
   thawed
   Cooking oil
1 small head lettuce, shredded
1 large tomato, chopped
1 cup shredded sharp American
   cheese (4 ounces)
   Creamy Russian salad dressing

In skillet cook beef, onion, and garlic till meat is browned and onion is tender. Drain off fat. Add chili powder and ½ teaspoon salt. Set aside and keep warm. In saucepan combine undrained green beans and kidney beans; heat and drain. In skillet fry tortillas, one at a time, on both sides in ¼ inch hot cooking oil till crisp, 30 to 45 seconds. Drain. Place tortillas in the center of dinner plates. Dividing ingredients equally, layer ingredients for tostadas in the following order: lettuce, beans, meat, tomato, and cheese. Serve at once. Pass Russian dressing. Serves 6.

Frenchy Beef Salad

3 cups cubed cooked potatoes
¼ cup French salad dressing
1½ cups cubed cooked beef
1 cup sliced celery
½ cup salad dressing or mayonnaise
½ cup sliced radishes
⅓ cup chili sauce
¼ cup dairy sour cream
2 tablespoons sliced green onion
1 tablespoon lemon juice
½ teaspoon salt
   Lettuce cups

In bowl combine potatoes and French dressing. Mix beef, celery, salad dressing, radishes, chili sauce, sour cream, onion, lemon juice, and salt; stir into potatoes. Cover and chill. Serve in lettuce cups. Serves 6.

Turkey-Orange Salad

⅓ cup lemon juice
⅓ cup salad oil
2 tablespoons snipped parsley
1 tablespoon chopped canned pimiento
1 tablespoon sugar
¼ teaspoon dry mustard
1 15-ounce can garbanzo beans, drained
1 small onion, thinly cut into rings

• • •

6 cups torn lettuce
2 cups cooked turkey cut into thin
    strips
1 11-ounce can mandarin orange
    sections, drained

In screw top jar combine lemon juice, salad oil, parsley, pimiento, sugar, mustard, and ½ teaspoon salt; cover and shake well. Pour over beans and onions; cover and chill 3 to 4 hours. Place lettuce, turkey, and oranges in large bowl. Add marinated vegetables with the dressing. Toss lightly to coat. Serves 6.

Turkey-Cranberry Aspic

1 envelope unflavored gelatin
⅓ cup cranberry juice cocktail
1 16-ounce can whole cranberry sauce
½ cup salad dressing or mayonnaise
½ cup whipping cream
½ cup chopped celery
6 ¼-inch-thick slices cooked white
    turkey meat
1½ teaspoons unflavored gelatin
1½ cups chicken broth

Soften the 1 envelope gelatin in the cranberry juice; stir over low heat till gelatin is dissolved. Break up cranberry sauce with a fork. Stir in dissolved gelatin. Blend in salad dressing. Whip cream just to soft peaks. Fold into gelatin mixture along with celery. Pour into 9x9x2-inch pan. Carefully place turkey slices atop. Chill till almost firm. Meanwhile, soften the 1½ teaspoons gelatin in chicken broth; stir over low heat till gelatin is dissolved. Cool the mixture. Carefully pour the gelatin-broth mixture over and around the turkey slices. Chill till firm. Makes 6 servings.

Yogurt-Chicken Salads

1 envelope unflavored gelatin
1¼ cups unsweetened pineapple juice
½ teaspoon salt
1 8-ounce carton lemon yogurt
¼ cup salad dressing or mayonnaise
1½ cups diced cooked chicken
¼ cup chopped celery
    Lettuce cups

In small saucepan soften unflavored gelatin in the unsweetened pineapple juice; add salt. Heat and stir till the gelatin is dissolved. Combine lemon yogurt and salad dressing or mayonnaise; stir in the gelatin.

Chill the yogurt mixture till partially set. Fold in diced chicken and chopped celery. Pour the mixture into 6 individual ½-cup molds; chill salad till firm. Unmold the salads in lettuce cups. Makes 6 servings.

Ham Mousse

2 envelopes unflavored
    gelatin
1 cup cold water
1 teaspoon dry mustard
1¼ cups chicken broth
2 beaten eggs
3 cups ground fully cooked ham
½ cup salad dressing or mayonnaise
2 tablespoons sliced green onion
1 teaspoon prepared horseradish
1 cup whipping cream
    Lettuce

Soften unflavored gelatin in cold water; set aside. Dissolve dry mustard in small amount of the chicken broth; combine with the remaining broth and beaten eggs in saucepan. Cook and stir over low heat till the mixture thickens slightly, 7 to 8 minutes. Add softened gelatin; stir till dissolved.

Beat in ground ham, salad dressing or mayonnaise, onion, and horseradish. Chill till the mixture is partially set. Whip the whipping cream; fold into ham mixture. Turn mixture into 6-cup mold. Chill the salad till set. Unmold salad onto lettuce-lined plate. Makes 8 to 10 servings.

Ham-Macaroni Salad

2½ cups elbow macaroni
1½ cups chopped fully cooked ham
1 cup bias-sliced celery
½ cup chopped onion
½ cup salad dressing or mayonnaise
2 tablespoons sweet pickle relish
2 teaspoons prepared mustard
Dash salt
Dash pepper
Lettuce cups
• • •
1 11-ounce can mandarin orange
sections, drained

In large saucepan cook macaroni in boiling salted water following package directions; drain and cool. Combine macaroni, ham, celery, and chopped onion. Blend together the salad dressing or mayonnaise, pickle relish, mustard, salt, and pepper. Stir lightly into ham mixture. Chill. Serve the salad in lettuce cups. Garnish the salad with mandarin orange sections. Makes 5 servings.

Super Ham Salad

8 cups torn lettuce
2 medium tomatoes, peeled and cut
in wedges
3 hard-cooked eggs, cut in wedges
1 small onion, sliced and separated
into rings
1 cup fully cooked ham cut in thin
strips
1 cup sharp American cheese
cut in narrow strips (4 ounces)
Salt
Pepper
• • •
¼ cup Italian salad dressing
¼ cup French salad dressing

In large salad bowl arrange torn lettuce, tomato wedges, hard-cooked eggs, onion rings, ham strips, and cheese. Sprinkle the salad with salt and pepper. Combine the Italian and French salad dressings in screw-top jar; cover and shake well. Pour dressing over salad and toss to coat. Makes 6 servings.

Main-Dish Salad Bowl

8 cups torn lettuce
3 cups torn spinach
1 12-ounce can luncheon meat, cut in
strips
2 tablespoons sliced green onion
2 tablespoons crumbled blue cheese
5 slices bacon, crisp-cooked, drained,
and crumbled
½ cup salad oil
⅓ cup wine vinegar
½ teaspoon sugar
½ teaspoon salt
½ teaspoon Worcestershire sauce
Dash pepper

In salad bowl combine lettuce, spinach, luncheon meat, onion, and crumbled blue cheese; chill. Before serving, add bacon to salad ingredients in bowl. In screw-top jar combine oil, vinegar, sugar, salt, Worcestershire, and pepper; cover and shake vigorously till blended. Pour over salad, tossing to coat all ingredients. Makes 6 servings.

Hot Sausage and Potato Salad

4 slices bacon
5 fully cooked smoked sausage links,
sliced
½ cup chopped onion
1 10½-ounce can condensed cream of
celery soup
¼ cup water
2 tablespoons sweet pickle relish
2 tablespoons vinegar
¼ teaspoon salt
1 16-ounce package frozen French-fried
potatoes

In skillet cook bacon till crisp. Drain, reserving 2 tablespoons drippings; set bacon aside. Cook sausage and onion in drippings till meat is browned and onion is tender, about 5 minutes. Stir in soup, water, pickle relish, vinegar, and salt; bring to boiling. Cut French-fried potatoes in half. Add potatoes to skillet and cook, covered, for 10 minutes, stirring once or twice. Crumble the reserved bacon over the top of the salad. Serves 4 to 6.

Hearty soups and stews

Cider Stew

2 pounds beef stew meat, cut in
    1-inch cubes
3 tablespoons cooking oil
3 tablespoons all-purpose flour
¼ teaspoon dried thyme, crushed
2 cups apple cider
2 tablespoons vinegar
3 potatoes, peeled and quartered
4 carrots, quartered
2 onions, sliced
1 stalk celery, sliced

In large saucepan brown the meat in hot oil.
Combine flour, thyme, 2 teaspoons salt, and
¼ teaspoon pepper; add to meat. Stir in cider,
vinegar, and ½ cup water. Cook and stir till
mixture boils. Reduce heat; simmer, covered,
till meat is tender, 1½ to 2 hours. Add remaining ingredients. Cook till vegetables are
tender, about 30 minutes. Serves 8.

Savory Meatball Soup

1 beaten egg
¼ cup milk
1 cup soft bread crumbs (2 slices)
½ teaspoon salt
½ pound ground beef
1 28-ounce can tomatoes
2 cups water
1½ cups chopped celery with leaves
1 cup finely chopped onion
1 cup diced potato
½ cup sliced carrot
1½ teaspoons salt
    Dash bottled hot pepper sauce
1 cup shredded American cheese

Combine first 4 ingredients. Add meat; mix
well. Chill 30 minutes. Meanwhile, in saucepan combine next 8 ingredients. Cover and
simmer 30 minutes. Shape meat into 16 meatballs; add to soup. Cover and simmer 10 minutes more. Serve soup in bowls; top with
cheese. Makes 8 servings.

Beef-Barley Soup

Place 2 pounds beef short ribs in large un-
heated saucepan; cook till browned on all
sides. Drain off fat. Add 5 cups water; one
16-ounce can tomatoes, cut up; 1 large onion,
sliced; and 1 tablespoon salt. Simmer, covered, for 1½ hours. Add 2 cups sliced carrot,
1 cup sliced celery, ¾ cup chopped green
pepper, ⅔ cup quick-cooking barley, and ¼
cup snipped parsley. Simmer, covered, 45
minutes more. Remove from heat. Cut meat
from ribs; cut meat into small pieces. Discard bones. Skim off fat from soup. Return
meat to soup; heat through. Serves 8 to 10.

Borscht

3 pounds beef shank cross cuts
2 medium onions, chopped
2 16-ounce cans whole beets
3 cups shredded cabbage
1 17-ounce can lima beans, drained
2 cups diced carrots
1 8-ounce can tomato sauce
3 tablespoons lemon juice
1 tablespoon sugar
2 teaspoons salt
⅛ teaspoon pepper

Cook beef in large saucepan till browned.
Add onions and 8 cups water; simmer, covered, till meat is tender, about 2 hours. Remove meat from bones. Discard bones. Skim
off excess fat from broth. Drain beets, reserving liquid; shred beets. Add beets and
liquid to broth along with meat, cabbage, and
remaining ingredients. Simmer till vegetables
are tender, 30 minutes. Serve hot. Serves 12.

An easy-on-the-budget stew

Meat, potatoes, carrots, onion, and celery sim- →
mered in apple cider give *Cider Stew* its rich
flavor. Serve it at your next family meal; you
are sure to win smiles of approval.

Devilish Beef Stew

1½ pounds beef stew meat, cut in
    1-inch cubes
⅓ cup all-purpose flour
2 tablespoons cooking oil
2 cups water
1 tablespoon dry mustard
1½ teaspoons salt
1 clove garlic, minced
1 teaspoon chili powder
1 teaspoon Worcestershire sauce
¼ teaspoon pepper
1½ cups water
4 medium potatoes, peeled and quartered
6 small onions, quartered
2 cups bias-sliced carrots
¼ cup cold water

Coat beef cubes with flour, reserving remaining flour. In a large saucepan or Dutch oven brown the beef, half at a time, in hot oil. Add the 2 cups water, mustard, salt, garlic, chili powder, Worcestershire, and pepper. Simmer, covered, till meat is almost tender, 1 to 1½ hours. Add the 1½ cups water, potatoes, onions, and carrots. Simmer, covered, till vegetables are tender, about 25 minutes.

For gravy, remove vegetables and skim fat from liquid, if necessary. Slowly blend ¼ cup cold water into the reserved flour till smooth. Stir slowly into hot liquid. Cook and stir till bubbly. Season to taste with salt and pepper. Return vegetables to gravy mixture. Heat through. Makes 8 servings.

Beef-Corn Soup

In large saucepan combine 2 pounds beef shank cross cuts, 6 cups water, 1 cup chopped onion, 1 cup chopped celery, 1 cup chopped carrot, 1 cup chopped peeled potato, 1 tablespoon salt, and dash pepper. Bring to boiling. Cover; simmer till beef is very tender, about 1½ hours. When cool, remove meat from bones; chop meat and return to soup. Discard bones. Add one undrained 16-ounce can cut green beans, one undrained 16-ounce can whole kernel corn, and ½ cup uncooked macaroni. Cover and simmer about 20 minutes. Season to taste. Makes 12 servings.

Oxtail Gumbo

3½ to 4 pounds beef oxtails
2 tablespoons margarine or butter
1¼ cups chopped celery
1 cup chopped onion
½ cup snipped parsley
2 teaspoons salt
½ teaspoon chili powder
½ teaspoon paprika
½ teaspoon dried thyme, crushed
1 16-ounce can tomatoes, cut up
1 10-ounce package frozen whole okra,
    thawed and sliced
1 teaspoon sugar

In large saucepan or Dutch oven brown the oxtails in margarine on all sides. Add 8 cups water, ¼ *cup* chopped celery, ½ *cup* chopped onion, parsley, salt, chili powder, paprika, thyme, and ¼ teaspoon pepper. Cover and simmer till meat is tender, about 2 hours. Chill; remove fat and strain broth. Remove meat from bones; chop meat and set aside. Discard bones. In large saucepan combine undrained tomatoes, okra, 1 cup celery, ½ cup onion, meat, broth, and sugar. Simmer, covered, 45 minutes. Serves 8 to 10.

Hearty Bean Soup

1 cup fully cooked ham cut in
    thin strips
½ cup chopped onion
1 clove garlic, minced
2 tablespoons cooking oil
1 16-ounce can tomatoes
1 14-ounce can Boston-style pork and
    beans in molasses sauce
¼ teaspoon salt
1 bay leaf
⅛ teaspoon dried thyme, crushed

In saucepan cook the ham, chopped onion, and garlic in hot oil till onion is tender. Place the undrained tomatoes and beans in blender container. Cover; blend till smooth. Add to the ham mixture. Stir in salt, bay leaf, and thyme; heat to boiling. Cook, covered, over low heat for 20 minutes, stirring occasionally. Remove the bay leaf. Makes 4 servings.

Sweet-Sour Pork Stew

¼ cup all-purpose flour
1 teaspoon salt
  Dash pepper

• • •

2 pounds boneless pork shoulder,
  cut in 1-inch cubes
2 tablespoons cooking oil
¼ cup packed brown sugar
1 tablespoon all-purpose flour
1 teaspoon salt
1 cup water
½ cup catsup
¼ cup vinegar
1 teaspoon Worcestershire sauce
1 cup chopped onion

In paper or plastic bag combine ¼ cup flour, 1 teaspoon salt, and the pepper. Add the pork cubes, a few at a time, shaking to coat with the seasoned flour. In large saucepan or Dutch oven brown the meat in hot oil. Combine brown sugar, flour, and 1 teaspoon salt. Stir in water, catsup, vinegar, and Worcestershire sauce. Stir mixture into the meat; add chopped onion. Cover and cook the stew over low heat for 1¾ hours, stirring occasionally. Makes 8 servings.

Arabian Lentil Soup

½ cup chopped onion
2 tablespoons margarine or butter
3 13¾-ounce cans chicken broth
½ cup bulgur wheat
½ cup canned garbanzo beans, drained
¼ cup dry lentils
  Dash pepper
2 tablespoons margarine or butter

In large saucepan or Dutch oven cook onion in 2 tablespoons margarine till tender but not brown. Add water to chicken broth to make 6 cups liquid. Add to saucepan along with bulgur wheat, garbanzo beans, lentils, and pepper. Simmer, covered, till lentils are tender (bulgur should still have some texture), 50 to 60 minutes. Just before serving, stir in 2 tablespoons margarine or butter. Season with salt, if desired. Makes 6 servings.

Chicken-Cheese Chowder

1 cup shredded carrot
¼ cup chopped onion
¼ cup margarine or butter
¼ cup all-purpose flour
2 cups milk
1 13¾-ounce can chicken broth
1 cup chopped cooked chicken
1 tablespoon dry white wine
½ teaspoon celery seed
½ teaspoon Worcestershire sauce

• • •

1 cup shredded sharp American cheese
  (4 ounces)
  Snipped chives

In a large saucepan or Dutch oven cook carrot and onion in margarine or butter till vegetables are tender but not brown. Blend in flour; add milk and chicken broth. Cook and stir till mixture is thickened and bubbly. Stir in chopped chicken, dry white wine, celery seed, and Worcestershire sauce. Cook till heated through. Add the shredded cheese; stir till cheese is melted. Garnish with snipped chives. Makes 4 or 5 servings.

Sausage-Bean Soup

¾ cup chopped onion
½ cup chopped green pepper
1 clove garlic, minced
2 tablespoons margarine or butter
2 15-ounce cans great northern beans
1 16-ounce can tomatoes, cut up
2 cups water
1 teaspoon salt
⅛ teaspoon pepper
2 4- or 5-ounce cans Vienna sausage,
  sliced *or* 6 frankfurters, sliced

In large saucepan or Dutch oven cook onion, green pepper, and garlic in margarine till tender but not brown. Add undrained beans, undrained tomatoes, water, salt, and pepper. Bring vegetables to boiling; reduce heat. Cover and simmer 10 to 15 minutes. Add the sliced sausages or frankfurters. Season soup to taste. Cover; simmer till heated through, about 5 minutes. Makes 8 to 10 servings.

Mulligatawny

¼ cup finely chopped onion
½ teaspoon curry powder
2 tablespoons shortening
1 cup diced cooked chicken
1 tart apple, peeled and chopped
¼ cup chopped carrot
¼ cup chopped celery
2 tablespoons chopped green pepper
3 tablespoons all-purpose flour
4 cups chicken broth
1 16-ounce can tomatoes, cut up
1 tablespoon snipped parsley
2 teaspoons lemon juice
1 teaspoon sugar
¼ teaspoon salt
2 whole cloves
Dash pepper

In large saucepan cook onion and curry powder in shortening till onion is tender but not brown. To cooked onion add chicken, apple, carrot, celery, and green pepper. Cook mixture, stirring occasionally, till vegetables are crisp-tender, about 5 minutes.

Sprinkle flour over chicken-vegetable mixture; stir to blend. Stir in chicken broth, undrained tomatoes, parsley, lemon juice, sugar, salt, whole cloves, and pepper. Bring the chicken-vegetable mixture to boiling, stirring occasionally. Reduce heat and simmer, covered, for 30 minutes. Makes 6 servings.

Turkey-Zucchini Soup

In large saucepan or Dutch oven cook 2 cups coarsely chopped zucchini and ½ cup chopped onion in 2 tablespoons margarine or butter till onion is tender but not brown. Add 2 cups water, one 9-ounce package frozen cut green beans, one 8-ounce can tomato sauce, 1 tablespoon instant chicken bouillon granules, 1 teaspoon Worcestershire sauce, ½ teaspoon salt, and dash pepper. Bring to boiling; simmer, uncovered, till beans are tender, about 15 minutes. Blend about 1 cup soup liquid into one 3-ounce package softened cream cheese; return to saucepan. Add 1½ cups chopped cooked turkey; heat the soup mixture through. Makes 5 or 6 servings.

Lamb Shanks and Bean Stew

1½ cups dry navy beans
6 lamb shank crosscuts
2 tablespoons cooking oil
½ cup chopped onion
2 cups sliced carrots
1 13¾-ounce can chicken broth
1 teaspoon salt
1 bay leaf
¼ teaspoon dried thyme, crushed
¼ teaspoon dried rosemary, crushed
Dash pepper
2 tablespoons all-purpose flour

Cover beans with 3½ cups water. Bring to boiling; simmer 2 minutes. Remove from heat; let stand 1 hour. Drain. Brown the shanks in hot oil for 25 to 30 minutes over medium heat; remove from pan. Drain off excess fat, reserving 2 tablespoons in skillet. Cook onion in drippings till tender. Stir in beans and remaining ingredients *except* flour. Place shanks on top. Bring to boiling. Cover and simmer till shanks and beans are tender, about 1½ hours. Remove shanks to platter. Remove bay leaf. Skim off excess fat. Blend ¼ cup cold water into flour. Stir into vegetables; bring to boiling. Makes 6 servings.

Lima Bean-Ham Chowder

1½ cups large dry lima beans
1 pound meaty ham hocks
1 cup chopped onion
½ cup chopped green pepper
2 tablespoons margarine or butter
2 cups milk
1 8¾-ounce can cream-style corn

Cover beans with 4 cups water. Bring to boiling; simmer 2 minutes. Remove from heat; let stand 1 hour. Add ham hocks; cover and simmer till tender, about 1½ hours. Add 1 teaspoon salt during last 30 minutes of cooking. Remove ham hocks. Mash beans slightly. Remove ham from bones; shred and set aside. Discard bones. Cook onion and green pepper in margarine till tender. Add to limas along with ham, milk, and corn. Heat, but do not boil. Season to taste. Makes 4 to 6 servings.

Black Bean Soup

1 cup dry black beans
1¼ cups beef broth
½ small green pepper, cut up
1 clove garlic, minced
½ teaspoon salt
½ teaspoon ground cumin seed
½ cup chopped pepperoni
    Sieved hard-cooked egg
    Dairy sour cream

Rinse beans; cover with 5 cups water. Bring to boiling; simmer 2 minutes. Remove from heat; let stand 1 hour. Bring beans back to boiling. Simmer beans 3 to 3½ hours. Drain beans, reserving liquid. In a blender container combine beans, beef broth, green pepper, garlic, salt, and cumin. Cover; blend till smooth (or mash and put through sieve). Place in a saucepan; add enough of reserved liquid to make of desired consistency, about 1¼ to 1½ cups (it should be like split pea soup). Stir in pepperoni and cook over low heat for 15 minutes, stirring frequently. Serve garnished with sieved hard-cooked egg and a dollop of sour cream. Makes 4 servings.

Mexican Rice and Bean Soup

1 12-ounce can luncheon meat, chopped
½ cup chopped onion
⅓ cup chopped green pepper
1 clove garlic, minced
2 tablespoons cooking oil
3 cups water
1 18-ounce can tomato juice
1 15½-ounce can red kidney beans
⅓ cup long grain rice
1 teaspoon paprika
½ to 1 teaspoon chili powder
½ teaspoon salt
    Dash pepper

In large saucepan cook luncheon meat, onion, green pepper, and garlic in hot oil till vegetables are tender but not brown. Add water, tomato juice, undrained beans, uncooked rice, paprika, chili powder, salt, and pepper. Simmer, covered, till rice is tender, 25 to 30 minutes, stirring occasionally. Serves 8.

Pinto Bean Chowder

2 cups dry pinto beans
6 cups water
4 teaspoons chicken-flavored
    gravy base
1 tablespoon instant minced onion
1 teaspoon salt
½ teaspoon fines herbes
    Dash pepper
        • • •
⅔ cup cold water
1 tablespoon all-purpose flour
1 5⅓-ounce can evaporated milk
6 slices bacon, crisp-cooked, drained,
    and crumbled

Rinse the pinto beans in cold water; place in large saucepan or Dutch oven with 6 cups water. Bring the beans to boiling; simmer 2 minutes. Remove from heat; let beans stand in water at least 1 hour. Add chicken-flavored gravy base, onion, salt, fines herbes, and pepper. Return the bean mixture to boiling. Reduce heat; cover and simmer till beans are tender, 1½ to 2 hours.

Slowly blend the ⅔ cup cold water into the flour; add with the evaporated milk to beans. Heat and stir till mixture just boils. Sprinkle soup with bacon. Makes 6 servings.

Smoky Corn Chowder

½ cup chopped onion
¼ cup margarine or butter
¼ cup all-purpose flour
1 teaspoon salt
⅛ teaspoon pepper
4 cups milk
1 17-ounce can whole kernel corn,
    drained
1 12-ounce package fully cooked smoked
    sausage links, sliced
1 8½-ounce can lima beans, drained

In saucepan cook onion in margarine or butter till tender but not brown. Blend in the flour, salt, and pepper. Add the milk all at once; cook and stir till thickened and bubbly. Stir in the corn, sausage, and lima beans. Simmer 10 minutes. Makes 6 servings.

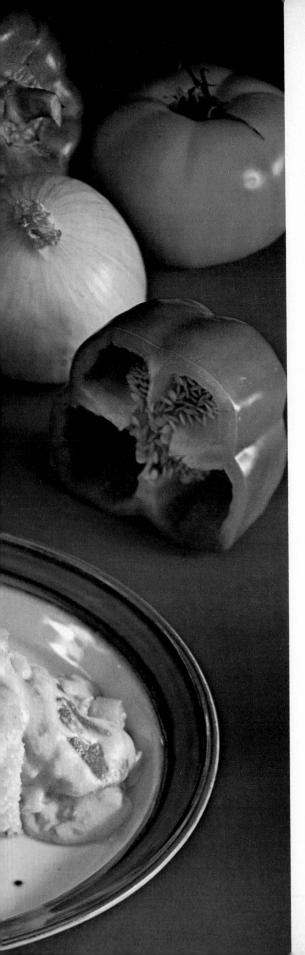

Pinch Hitters for Meat

Meat stretching is a lot like baseball. Just as coaches sometimes substitute a pinch hitter for a starting player, homemakers must learn to occasionally substitute different forms of protein for meat. An economical way to stretch the meat dollar is to plan some meals around fish, eggs, cheese, or vegetables such as dry beans or peanut butter. These foods will replace the protein you would get in meat, often at a lower cost. Use them alone or in combination with a little meat. Using pinch hitters for meat at one meal allows you to feature a more expensive meat at another.

The recipes in this section will show you that dishes without meat can be attractive and satisfying. Choose from a large selection of main dishes, salads, sandwiches, and soups.

Try *Chinese Tuna Casserole* (see recipe, page 88) and *Cheese-Tomato Shortcake* (see recipe, page 96). These appetizing meat pinch hitter recipes will stretch your food dollar.

Budget-worthy main dishes

The money-saving recipes in this section are based on fish, cheese, and eggs. Saving money on these meat pinch hitters is easy if you shop wisely. Here are a few helpful shopping suggestions:

Fish: Choose the form—fresh, frozen, or canned—that best suits your cooking needs. Use fresh or frozen fish in recipes that call for large pieces of fish. Canned fish such as tuna and salmon are the most economical in casseroles, sandwiches, or salads.

When buying whole fish, look for freshness. The flesh should be elastic, yet firm. The eyes should be clear, and bulging. For frozen fish, check to make sure the fish is solidly frozen and the package is sealed tightly.

The best buys in canned fish are tuna and salmon. Manufacturers pack tuna according to the size of the pieces. For casseroles choose chunk tuna because the pieces hold their shape. For sandwich fillings flaked tuna works well because the fish is already in small pieces. Save the more expensive solid-pack tuna for special occasions.

When buying salmon, check the label for the color of the fish. Pink salmon is the most economical. It works best in loaves and patties because it breaks into flakes. The more expensive deep red salmon breaks into large chunks and is attractive in salads.

Eggs: Save money on eggs by noticing grade. The U.S. grades for eggs are AA, A, and B. The higher grades, AA and A, work well in most dishes, while grade B eggs, should be used in dishes that call for beaten eggs.

The egg size (jumbo, extra large, large, medium, small, and peewee) is also important. As a rule, remember that if there is less than seven cents difference in price per dozen between one size and the next in the same grade, you will save money by buying the larger size.

Cheese: Save on cheese by buying whole pieces. Then slice, shred, or grate it yourself. In this way, you save the cost of handling and packaging. Also compare the prices of natural and process varieties. Often, process cheeses cost less than natural ones.

Chinese Tuna Casserole

This tasty meat-stretching recipe is shown on page 86—

> 1 3-ounce can chow mein
>   noodles
> 1 6½- or 7-ounce can tuna, drained
>   and flaked
> 1 cup sliced celery
> ¼ cup chopped onion
> ¼ cup chopped green pepper
> • • •
> 1 10¾-ounce can condensed cream of
>   mushroom soup
> ⅔ cup water

Reserve ¼ *cup* of the chow mein noodles; combine the remaining chow mein noodles with flaked tuna, sliced celery, chopped onion, and chopped green pepper. Stir together cream of mushroom soup and water. Stir in tuna-vegetable mixture. Turn into 1-quart casserole; sprinkle with the remaining ¼ cup noodles. Bake, uncovered, at 350° for 35 to 40 minutes. Serves 4.

Sweet-Sour Tuna

> 1 10½-ounce can chicken gravy
> 1 medium green pepper, cut into ¾-
>   inch squares
> ¼ cup sugar
> 2 tablespoons vinegar
> 2 tablespoons soy sauce
> 1 13¼-ounce can pineapple tidbits,
>   drained
> 1 9¼-ounce can tuna, drained and
>   broken into chunks
>   Hot cooked rice

In medium saucepan bring chicken gravy, green pepper squares, sugar, vinegar, and soy sauce to boiling. Reduce heat; cover and simmer 8 minutes, stirring occasionally. Add pineapple tidbits and tuna. Cook and stir till heated through, about 2 minutes more. Serve over hot cooked rice. Makes 4 servings.

Tuna-Broccoli Casserole

1 10-ounce package frozen chopped
    broccoli
3 tablespoons margarine or butter
¼ cup all-purpose flour
1¾ cups milk
3 tablespoons grated Parmesan cheese
1 tablespoon lemon juice
    Dash dried dillweed
1 6½- or 7-ounce can tuna, drained
    and broken into chunks
1 package refrigerated biscuits
    (6 biscuits)

Cook broccoli according to package directions; drain and set aside. Over low heat melt margarine; blend in flour and ¼ teaspoon salt. Add milk all at once. Cook and stir till thickened and bubbly. Add Parmesan, lemon juice, and dillweed. Fold in tuna and cooked broccoli. Turn into 1½-quart casserole. Bake, covered, at 375° for 15 minutes. Arrange refrigerated biscuits around edge of casserole; bake 15 minutes more. Makes 4 to 6 servings.

Hot Tuna Bake

An easy, yet hearty fix-up —

2 cups water
1¾ cups White Sauce Mix (see recipe,
    page 19)
¼ cup chopped celery
1 teaspoon instant minced onion
½ teaspoon salt
1 6½- or 7-ounce can tuna, drained
    and flaked
3 hard-cooked eggs, chopped
¼ cup chopped pimiento-stuffed
    green olives
⅓ cup fine dry bread crumbs
1 tablespoon margarine, melted

In saucepan combine water, White Sauce Mix, celery, onion, salt, and dash pepper. Cook and stir till thickened; cook 2 minutes longer. Add tuna, hard-cooked eggs, and olives. Spoon into 6 individual baking shells. Combine bread crumbs and melted margarine; sprinkle over tuna mixture. Bake at 350° for 15 to 20 minutes. Serves 6.

Tomato-Perch Casserole

Thaw one 1-pound package frozen perch fillets. Place in skillet with enough water to cover. Simmer, covered, just till fish flakes, 5 to 8 minutes. Drain well; cut into ½-inch pieces. Set aside. In saucepan melt 2 tablespoons margarine or butter; blend in ¼ cup all-purpose flour, 1 teaspoon instant chicken bouillon granules, and ¼ teaspoon salt. Add 1¾ cups milk all at once. Cook and stir till thickened and bubbly. Add ½ cup shredded sharp American cheese (4 ounces); stir to melt. Add fish to creamed mixture.

Peel, seed, and dice 2 medium tomatoes. Stir into creamed mixture. Pour into five 8-ounce casserole dishes; top with an additional ¼ cup shredded sharp American cheese. Sprinkle with paprika. Bake at 350° till mixture is hot, 10 to 15 minutes. Serves 5.

Scalloped Fish

1 1-pound package frozen fish fillets,
    thawed and cut in 1-inch pieces
2 cups water
¼ cup finely chopped onion
¼ cup finely chopped green pepper
1 tablespoon margarine or butter,
    melted
2 beaten eggs
1½ cups milk
1½ cups coarsely crumbled saltine
    crackers (20 crackers)
1 16-ounce can peas and carrots,
    drained
1 tablespoon lemon juice
2 teaspoons Worcestershire sauce
⅛ teaspoon pepper
½ cup shredded sharp American cheese
    (2 ounces)

Place fish in water. Simmer, covered, 3 minutes; drain thoroughly. Cook onion and green pepper in margarine till tender. Combine eggs, milk, and cracker crumbs. Stir in cooked fish, onion, green pepper, peas and carrots, lemon juice, Worcestershire, and pepper. Turn into 2-quart casserole. Bake at 350° till set, about 50 minutes. Sprinkle with cheese and bake 5 minutes more. Serves 6.

Pear-Salmon Squares

    1 29-ounce can pear halves (8 halves)
    1 6-ounce package lemon-flavored
        gelatin
    2 tablespoons lemon juice
    ¾ cup dairy sour cream
    1 7¾-ounce can salmon, drained, bones
        and skin removed, and flaked
    ¼ cup finely chopped celery

Drain pears, reserving syrup; add water to syrup to make 3 cups. Bring to boiling. Add gelatin; stir till dissolved. Add lemon juice. *To half* the mixture, add ½ cup sour cream; beat till smooth. Pour into 9x9x2-inch pan. To remaining gelatin, add ⅓ cup water. Chill both mixtures till partially set. Combine salmon, celery, and the remaining sour cream; mound into cut side of pears. Press pears, filled side up, into sour cream-gelatin mixture. Spoon remaining clear gelatin around pears. Chill till firm. Serves 8.

Saucy Salmon Loaf

    1 cup finely chopped celery
    ¼ cup finely chopped onion
    2 beaten eggs
    1 16-ounce can salmon, drained, bones
        and skin removed, and mashed
    1 cup finely crushed saltine
        crackers (about 22 crackers)
    2 tablespoons sweet pickle relish
    1 cup milk
    2 tablespoons all-purpose flour
    Cheese Sauce

Combine celery, onion, and 2 tablespoons water. Cook, covered, for 5 minutes; drain. Mix together eggs, cooked vegetables, salmon, crackers, relish, and 1 teaspoon salt; mix well. In saucepan blend together milk and flour; cook and stir till thickened and bubbly. Cook 1 minute more. Stir in salmon mixture. Shape into loaf; place in 11x7½x1½-inch baking pan. Bake at 350° for about 40 minutes. Serve with Cheese Sauce. Serves 6.

    Cheese Sauce: In saucepan combine one 10¾-ounce can condensed Cheddar cheese soup and ⅓ cup milk. Heat through.

Dilled Salmon Pie

    1 beaten egg
    ½ cup milk
    2 cups soft bread crumbs (2½ slices)
    1 tablespoon chopped onion
    1 tablespoon margarine or butter,
        melted
    ½ teaspoon salt
    1 16-ounce can salmon, drained, bones
        and skin removed, and flaked
    Packaged instant mashed potatoes
        (enough for 4 servings)
    1 egg
    Dill Sauce

Mix together egg, milk, crumbs, onion, margarine, and salt till crumbs are moistened. Add salmon and mix well. Turn into greased 8-inch pie plate. Prepare instant potatoes according to package directions, *omitting milk.* Beat in the remaining egg. Spoon around edge of pie. Bake at 350° for 30 to 35 minutes. Pass Dill Sauce. Serves 4 to 6.

    Dill Sauce: Melt 1 tablespoon margarine. Blend in 1 tablespoon all-purpose flour. Stir in 1¼ cups milk, 1 teaspoon sugar, ¾ teaspoon dried dillweed, and ½ teaspoon salt. Cook and stir till thickened and bubbly. Combine ½ cup dairy sour cream and 1 tablespoon lemon juice. Gradually stir into hot mixture. Heat through but do not boil.

Clam Fritters

    2 well-beaten egg yolks
    ½ cup milk
    2 7½-ounce cans minced clams, drained
    1 cup fine dry bread crumbs
    2 teaspoons snipped parsley
    1 teaspoon salt
    ½ teaspoon pepper
    2 stiffly beaten egg whites
    Cooking oil

Combine beaten egg yolks, milk, clams, bread crumbs, parsley, salt, and pepper. Fold in stiffly beaten egg whites. Drop batter from a tablespoon into skillet containing ¼ inch hot oil. Fry, turning once. Garnish with orange slices, if desired. Makes 6 servings.

Clam Chowder Casserole

2 10-ounce packages frozen cauliflower
½ cup chopped onion
½ cup chopped celery
¼ cup margarine or butter
¼ cup all-purpose flour
¾ teaspoon salt
⅛ teaspoon pepper
2 cups milk
1 teaspoon instant chicken bouillon granules
2 7½-ounce cans minced clams, drained
2 tablespoons chopped canned pimiento
1 package refrigerated biscuits (6 biscuits)
2 tablespoons margarine or butter, melted
2 tablespoons grated Parmesan cheese

In saucepan cook frozen cauliflower according to package directions. Drain well; cut up large pieces. Meanwhile, cook onion and celery in ¼ cup margarine till tender but not brown. Blend in flour, salt, and pepper. Add milk and chicken bouillon granules. Cook and stir till thickened and bubbly. Add cooked cauliflower, clams, and pimiento; bring to boiling. Turn into 2-quart casserole. Halve refrigerated biscuits. Brush with the 2 tablespoons melted margarine; sprinkle with Parmesan cheese. Place atop *hot* mixture. Bake at 450° for 15 minutes. Makes 6 servings.

Shrimp and Green Bean Bake

Drain and thoroughly rinse one 4½-ounce can shrimp. Cook one 9-ounce package frozen French-style green beans according to package directions, *omitting salt;* drain thoroughly. Place green beans in a 1-quart casserole. Cover with shrimp. Combine one 10½-ounce can condensed cream of celery soup, 2 tablespoons snipped parsley, ¼ teaspoon grated lemon peel, and 1 teaspoon lemon juice; pour mixture over shrimp. Cover and bake at 350° for 15 minutes. Uncover and top with ½ cup shredded American cheese (2 ounces). Sprinkle with paprika, if desired, and bake till mixture is hot and cheese is melted, 5 to 10 minutes more. Serves 5.

Chip and Cheese Scallops

1 pound fresh or frozen scallops
1 tablespoon finely chopped onion
3 tablespoons margarine or butter
3 tablespoons all-purpose flour
⅛ teaspoon pepper
½ cup milk
1 3-ounce can chopped mushrooms, drained
2 tablespoons grated Parmesan cheese
2 tablespoons chopped canned pimiento
1 tablespoon snipped parsley
½ cup shredded sharp American cheese
1½ cups crushed potato chips

Thaw frozen scallops; rinse. Cover scallops with cold water. Bring to boiling; reduce heat and simmer 2 minutes. Drain, reserving 1 cup liquid. Slice scallops about ¼ inch thick.

Cook onion in margarine till tender. Blend in flour and pepper. Add reserved cooking liquid and milk. Cook and stir till thickened. Remove from heat. Stir in next 4 ingredients and scallops. Turn into 1½-quart casserole; sprinkle with shredded cheese and top with potato chips. Bake at 350° for 20 to 25 minutes. Serves 5 or 6.

Oyster-Rice Casserole

⅔ cup long grain rice
½ cup finely chopped celery
¼ cup finely chopped onion
1 13-ounce can evaporated milk
⅓ cup Seasoned Coating Mix (see recipe, page 18)
2 tablespoons margarine or butter, melted
1 5-ounce can oysters, drained

Cook rice according to package directions. Cook celery and onion, covered, in ¼ cup water till crisp-tender. Combine undrained vegetables, cooked rice, and evaporated milk. Turn into 1-quart casserole. Bake at 400° for 15 minutes, stirring once. Mix Seasoned Coating Mix and margarine in plastic bag. Add oysters; shake to coat. Place oysters and remaining coating mixture over rice. Bake 15 minutes more. Serves 4.

Three-Cheese Manicotti

    1 8-ounce can tomato sauce
    1 envelope spaghetti sauce mix
    2 cups shredded mozzarella cheese
    1 cup cream-style cottage cheese
    ½ cup grated Parmesan cheese
    2 beaten eggs
    ¼ cup snipped parsley
    ½ teaspoon salt
    ⅛ teaspoon pepper
    8 manicotti shells, cooked and drained

Blend tomato sauce, spaghetti sauce mix, and 1½ cups water. Simmer, uncovered, 10 to 12 minutes. Meanwhile, combine *1 cup* of the mozzarella, the cottage cheese, and Parmesan. Add eggs, parsley, salt, and pepper; mix lightly. Stuff manicotti shells with cheese mixture, using about ¼ cup for each. Pour ½ *cup* of the sauce mixture into 12x7½x2-inch baking dish. Arrange manicotti in dish; pour remaining sauce atop. Sprinkle with remaining mozzarella. Bake, uncovered, at 350° till bubbly, 25 to 30 minutes. Serves 6.

Swiss Stuffed Green Peppers

    1 cup long grain rice
    6 medium green peppers
    8 slices bacon
    ½ cup chopped onion
    • • •
    1 beaten egg
    1½ cups shredded Swiss cheese
    ⅓ cup milk
    2 tablespoons chopped canned pimiento

Cook rice according to package directions. Cut off tops of peppers; remove seeds and membrane. Precook pepper shells in boiling salted water 5 minutes; drain. Sprinkle pepper cavities with salt. Cook bacon till crisp; drain and crumble, reserving 2 tablespoons drippings in skillet. Cook onion in reserved drippings till tender. Combine remaining ingredients, rice, onion, and *3 tablespoons* of the crumbled bacon. Spoon mixture into peppers. Sprinkle with remaining bacon. Place peppers in shallow baking dish. Bake at 350° for 25 minutes. Serves 6.

Swiss Cheese Bake

    1 tablespoon instant minced onion
    2 tablespoons margarine, softened
    2 teaspoons prepared mustard
    2 teaspoons sesame seeds, toasted
    6 slices white bread
    5 slices Swiss cheese (5 ounces)
    4 beaten eggs
    2 cups milk

Soak onion in 1 tablespoon water; blend in margarine, mustard, and *1 teaspoon* of the sesame seeds. Spread mixture on one side of bread slices. Alternately layer bread and cheese slices, forming 2 stacks. Quarter each stack diagonally, making a total of 8 triangles; arrange triangles in 9x9x2-inch baking pan, placing crust edge down. Beat together eggs and milk; pour slowly over bread and cheese. Sprinkle remaining sesame seeds atop. Let stand 10 minutes. Bake at 350° for 40 to 45 minutes. Let stand 5 minutes before serving. Makes 6 servings.

Cheesy Rice Casserole

Cook ½ cup chopped onion and ¼ cup chopped green pepper in 2 tablespoons margarine or butter till tender but not brown. Cook 1 cup long grain rice according to package directions. Combine rice with 1 cup cream-style cottage cheese, 1 beaten egg, 2 tablespoons chopped canned pimiento, the cooked vegetables, and ½ teaspoon salt. Spoon *half* the mixture into a 1½-quart casserole. Cover with 2 sliced hard-cooked eggs and sprinkle with ½ cup shredded American cheese (2 ounces). Spread remaining rice mixture atop and sprinkle with another ½ cup shredded American cheese (2 ounces). Cover and bake at 375° for 25 to 30 minutes. Sprinkle with paprika. Makes 6 servings.

An Italian favorite without meat

For a switch from spaghetti try *Three-Cheese →
Manicotti.* Serve this dish with a tossed salad, toasted French bread, and red wine. For extra richness pass additional grated Parmesan.

Cheesy Egg Pizza

  1 package active dry yeast
  ¾ cup warm water (110°)
2½ cups Basic Biscuit Mix (see recipe,
     page 20)
    Cooking oil
  8 hard-cooked eggs, sliced
  1 15-ounce can tomato sauce
  ¼ cup sliced green onion
  ¼ cup chopped green pepper
  1 teaspoon dried oregano, crushed
  ½ teaspoon dried thyme, crushed
  ⅛ teaspoon garlic powder
    Dash pepper
  1 cup shredded mozzarella cheese
    Dried crushed red pepper

Soften yeast in warm water. Add the Basic Biscuit Mix; beat vigorously for 2 minutes. Knead dough till smooth (25 strokes) on a surface sprinkled lightly with flour. Divide dough in half; cover and let rest 10 minutes. Roll out each half of the dough and fit into a greased 12-inch pizza pan. Crimp edges. Brush dough lightly with cooking oil. Bake at 425° for 10 minutes.

Remove from oven. Arrange *half* the egg slices on each of the pizza crusts. Combine remaining ingredients *except* cheese and red pepper; spread *half* the mixture over the eggs on each pizza. Sprinkle cheese over all. Bake at 425° till crusts are done, 5 to 7 minutes. Pass the dried crushed red pepper to sprinkle on pizza. Makes 6 to 8 servings.

Use cheese and egg main dishes

Eggs and cheese are excellent sources of protein. In fact, either can stand on its own to provide many of the nutrients found in meats—at less cost. You can plan nutritious, satisfying main dishes using as little as ½ cup cheese or 2 eggs per serving. Serve these economical protein sources in a wide variety of main dishes, sandwiches, main dish salads, and soups.

Cheese-Parsley Soufflé

  ¾ cup White Sauce Mix (see recipe,
     page 19)
  2 cups shredded sharp American cheese
  ½ cup Seasoned Rice Mix (see recipe,
     page 21)
  ¼ cup finely snipped parsley
  4 egg yolks
  4 egg whites
  1 10¾-ounce can condensed cream of
     mushroom soup
  ½ cup dairy sour cream

Combine the White Sauce Mix and 1 cup water. Cook and stir till thickened and bubbly. Remove from heat; stir in cheese. Prepare Seasoned Rice Mix according to recipe directions. Add prepared rice mix and parsley to cheese sauce. Beat egg yolks till thick and lemon-colored; stir in a moderate amount of hot mixture, then return to remaining hot mixture. Beat egg whites till stiff peaks form; fold into cheese-rice mixture. Pour into *ungreased* 10x6x2-inch baking dish. Bake at 325° till knife inserted off-center comes out clean, 35 to 40 minutes. Meanwhile, combine soup and sour cream; heat through but do not boil. Serve over soufflé. Makes 6 servings.

Mexican Omelet

  1 small tomato, chopped and drained
  ¼ cup salad dressing or mayonnaise
  2 tablespoons chopped canned green
     chili peppers
  1 tablespoon chopped green onion
  1 teaspoon lemon juice
  2 tablespoons margarine or butter
  2 corn tortillas, torn in pieces
  8 beaten eggs
  1 cup shredded Monterey Jack cheese

Combine first 5 ingredients and ¼ teaspoon salt. Heat mixture to boiling; remove from heat and keep warm. In 10-inch skillet melt margarine; cook tortillas till soft. Pour in eggs; cook 3 to 5 minutes, lifting to allow uncooked mixture to flow under. Sprinkle with cheese. Fold omelet in half on warm plate. Spoon sauce over omelet. Serves 6.

Make an *Apple Omelet* the next time you are looking for a different idea in omelets. Start by fixing a tasty, fresh apple filling, and if desired, use smoky sausage for a special flavor bonus.

Apple Omelet

¼ cup packed brown sugar
1 tablespoon cornstarch
⅔ cup cold water
2 teaspoons lemon juice
3 apples, peeled, cored, and cut in
    ½-inch-thick wedges (3 cups)
2 tablespoons margarine or butter
3 fully cooked smoked sausage links,
    sliced diagonally (optional)
4 egg whites
4 egg yolks
1 tablespoon margarine or butter

In saucepan combine brown sugar and cornstarch. Stir in ⅔ cup cold water and lemon juice. Cook quickly, stirring constantly, till thickened and bubbly. Add apples and stir gently. Cover and simmer gently till apples are tender, 3 to 5 minutes. Add the 2 tablespoons margarine. Add sausage, if desired.

Stir till margarine melts. Keep warm. Beat egg whites till frothy; add 2 tablespoons water and ¼ teaspoon salt. Beat egg whites till stiff, but not dry peaks form. Beat egg yolks till very thick and lemon-colored. Gently fold yolks into whites.

Heat the 1 tablespoon margarine in 10-inch oven-going skillet till a drop of water sizzles when dropped into the hot fat. Pour in omelet mixture and spread evenly with spatula, leaving high at sides. Cook over low heat till lightly browned, 8 to 10 minutes. Bake at 325° till knife inserted off-center comes out clean, 8 to 10 minutes. Loosen sides of omelet with spatula. Make shallow cut across omelet slightly above and parallel to skillet handle. Tilt pan. Fold upper (smaller) half over lower half. Using spatula, slip omelet onto hot serving platter. Fill center of omelet with the hot apple-sausage mixture, *reserving ½ cup* mixture. Pour the reserved mixture over the top. Makes 4 servings.

Bacon-Rice Omelet

In an 8-inch skillet cook 2 slices bacon till crisp; drain, reserving 1 tablespoon drippings in skillet. Crumble bacon; set aside. Cook ¼ cup chopped celery in the drippings till tender. Remove skillet from heat. Prepare 1 cup Seasoned Rice Mix (see recipe, page 21) according to the recipe directions. Combine 4 beaten eggs, prepared rice, ¼ cup milk, ¼ teaspoon salt, and dash pepper. Pour into skillet. Top with ½ cup shredded American cheese (2 ounces) and crumbled bacon. Cover; cook over low heat till done, 15 to 16 minutes. Loosen omelet. Cut in wedges to serve. Makes 4 servings.

Cheese-Tomato Shortcake

This superb main dish is shown on page 86 —

    Corn Bread
  1 cup chopped celery
  ½ cup chopped onion
  2 tablespoons margarine or butter
  2 tablespoons all-purpose flour
  1 16-ounce can tomatoes, cut up
  ¼ cup water
  ½ teaspoon salt
  ½ teaspoon dried oregano, crushed
  ¼ teaspoon garlic salt
  5 or 6 drops bottled hot pepper sauce
  2 cups shredded sharp American cheese

Prepare and bake Corn Bread. Meanwhile, cook celery and onion in margarine till tender; blend in flour. Stir in the remaining ingredients *except* cheese. Heat and stir till mixture is thickened and bubbly. Remove from heat; add cheese. Stir to melt. To serve, split corn bread squares in half; spoon the tomato mixture between and over top. Makes 8 servings.

Corn Bread: Stir to combine thoroughly 1 cup all-purpose flour, 1 cup yellow cornmeal, ¼ cup sugar, 4 teaspoons baking powder, and ¾ teaspoon salt. Add 2 beaten eggs, 1 cup milk, and ¼ cup cooking oil. Beat with electric or rotary beater just till smooth, about 1 minute. (Don't overbeat.) Bake in greased 9x9x2-inch baking pan at 425° for 15 to 20 minutes. Cut into 8 squares.

Zucchini Italiano

  6 small zucchini, cut in ¼-inch slices
     (about 6¾ cups)
  ½ cup chopped onion
  ¼ cup chopped green pepper
  2 tablespoons margarine or butter
  1 15-ounce can tomato sauce
  ¾ teaspoon dried basil, crushed
  ½ teaspoon dried thyme, crushed
  ¼ teaspoon salt
  2 hard-cooked eggs
  1 6-ounce package sliced mozzarella
     cheese
  6 slices bacon, crisp-cooked, drained,
     and crumbled

In large saucepan cook zucchini, covered, in boiling salted water till crisp-tender, about 5 minutes. Drain well. Cook onion and green pepper in margarine till tender but not brown. Stir in tomato sauce, basil, thyme, and salt; heat through. Remove yolks from hard-cooked eggs; set aside. Chop egg whites and add to tomato mixture. In 11x7½x1½-inch baking dish layer the zucchini, *half* the tomato sauce, the cheese slices, the remaining tomato sauce, and crumbled bacon. Bake at 350° till heated through, 15 to 20 minutes. Sieve egg yolks and sprinkle atop. Makes 6 servings.

Easy Potato Pancakes

Serve these pancakes with warmed applesauce —

  3 cups frozen loose-pack hashed brown
     potatoes, thawed
  ¼ cup all-purpose flour
  1½ teaspoons instant minced onion
     Dash white pepper
  3 beaten eggs
  ¼ cup milk
  2 tablespoons cooking oil

In bowl combine first 4 ingredients and 2 teaspoons salt. Combine eggs, milk, and oil; stir into potato mixture. Let potato batter stand 5 minutes. Drop batter in ¼-cup portions onto a hot greased griddle. When underside is browned, turn and brown the other side. Makes 10 pancakes.

Mexican Lima Beans

2½ cups large dry lima beans
1 15-ounce can tomato sauce
1 medium onion, sliced
⅓ cup chili sauce
¼ cup chopped green pepper
1 teaspoon chili powder
1 cup dairy sour cream
¼ cup shredded American cheese
½ cup crushed corn chips

Rinse beans; add to 8 cups cold water in saucepan. Bring to boiling and simmer 2 minutes. Remove from heat and cover; let stand 1 hour. (Or add beans to water; soak overnight.) Cover beans; simmer over low heat (do not boil) till just tender, 30 to 40 minutes. Drain, reserving 1 cup bean liquid.

In 2-quart casserole combine beans and reserved liquid, tomato sauce, onion, chili sauce, green pepper, chili powder, and 1 teaspoon salt. Cover and bake at 300° for 2½ hours. Spread sour cream over the top; sprinkle with cheese. Sprinkle corn chips around edge. Bake 5 minutes more. Serves 8.

Individual Spinach Casseroles

2 10-ounce packages frozen chopped
    spinach
2 tablespoons margarine or butter
¼ cup all-purpose flour
    Milk
1½ cups shredded American cheese
1 cup milk
4 beaten eggs
¼ cup finely chopped onion
½ teaspoon dried oregano, crushed
⅛ teaspoon salt
⅛ teaspoon pepper

Cook spinach according to package directions. Drain, reserving liquid. Melt margarine; blend in flour. Add milk to reserved spinach liquid to equal 1 cup; add to flour mixture. Cook and stir till thickened. Stir in remaining ingredients. Cook and stir till cheese melts. Spoon into six 1-cup casseroles. Bake at 350° till knife inserted off-center comes out clean, 20 to 25 minutes. Serves 6.

Tomato Dumplings

2 cups Basic Biscuit Mix (see recipe,
    page 20)
1 cup cream-style cottage cheese,
    drained
2 hard-cooked eggs, chopped
2 tablespoons finely chopped onion
1 tablespoon snipped parsley
3 small tomatoes, peeled and
    quartered
1 tablespoon margarine or butter
1 tablespoon all-purpose flour
⅔ cup milk
½ cup shredded American cheese

Combine Basic Biscuit Mix and ½ cup water. Knead dough a few strokes on a surface sprinkled lightly with flour. Roll into a 12-inch square. Cut in four 6-inch squares. Combine next 4 ingredients. Spoon a generous ⅓ cup of the cheese mixture on each square. Place 3 tomato wedges atop. Season with salt and pepper. Moisten edges of dough. Bring corners of dough to center; pinch edges to seal. Place in a greased 15½x10½x1-inch baking pan. Bake at 425° till golden, about 15 minutes. Melt margarine; stir in flour and ⅛ teaspoon salt. Add milk; cook and stir till thickened. Stir in cheese. Cook and stir till cheese melts. Serve cheese sauce over the dumplings. Makes 4 servings.

Use vegetables as main dishes

Vegetable main dishes are nutritious, low in cost, and delicious. Some vegetables such as tomatoes and spinach are low in protein, so you'll need to combine them with cheese and eggs. However, other vegetables such as peanuts, dry beans, and soybeans* are good sources of protein and as such can stand alone in a main dish.

You can supplement the protein in your vegetable main dishes by serving milk and bread with the meal.

*See the tip box on page 36 for the special uses of soybeans.

Sandwiches and main dish salads

Cheese-Tuna Sandwiches

  1 6½- or 7-ounce can tuna, drained
    and flaked
  1 cup diced American cheese
  ½ cup salad dressing or mayonnaise
  1 hard-cooked egg, chopped
  ¼ cup sweet pickle relish
  2 tablespoons chopped onion
  1 tablespoon chopped canned pimiento
    Margarine or butter, softened
  8 frankfurter buns, split and toasted

In bowl combine first 7 ingredients. Spread margarine on frankfurter buns. Spread tuna mixture on bottom half of buns. Broil 3 to 4 inches from heat till cheese is melted and tuna is heated through, about 2 minutes. Top with remaining bun half. Makes 8 sandwiches.

Tomato-Sardine Sandwiches

  1 8-ounce can sardines in tomato
    sauce, chilled
  ½ cup shredded American cheese
  2 hard-cooked eggs, chopped
  ¼ cup finely chopped celery
  2 tablespoons catsup
  1 tablespoon lemon juice
    Margarine or butter, softened
  12 slices white bread
    Lettuce

Mash sardines. Add shredded cheese, eggs, celery, catsup, and lemon juice. Set aside. Spread margarine on bread slices. Spread sardine mixture on 6 slices of the bread. Top with lettuce and remaining 6 slices of bread. Makes 6 sandwiches.

A colorful sandwich favorite

← *Fiesta Sandwich Rolls* are ideal for after-the-game entertaining. Make the sandwich rolls ahead of time, then heat them just before serving. They are delicious with glasses of milk.

Hot Salmon Sandwiches

  1 7¾-ounce can salmon, drained, bones
    and skin removed, and flaked
  ⅓ cup salad dressing or mayonnaise
  ⅓ cup chopped celery
  3 tablespoons sweet pickle relish
  1 teaspoon lemon juice
  ⅛ teaspoon pepper
          • • •
  10 slices white bread
  1 egg
  ½ cup milk
    Dash salt
    Margarine or butter

Combine salmon, salad dressing, celery, relish, lemon juice, and pepper. Spread on *5 slices* of bread; top with remaining 5 slices. Beat together egg, milk, and salt. Dip each sandwich in egg mixture. In skillet cook sandwiches in melted margarine over medium heat till both sides are golden, about 5 minutes per side. Makes 5 sandwiches.

Fiesta Sandwich Rolls

  2 cups shredded sharp
    American cheese (8 ounces)
  4 hard-cooked eggs, chopped
  ½ cup tomato sauce
  ¼ cup chopped pitted ripe olives
  2 tablespoons chopped canned green
    chili peppers
  2 tablespoons sliced green onion
  4 teaspoons vinegar
    Dash garlic salt
  6 large hard rolls

Combine cheese, hard-cooked eggs, tomato sauce, olives, chili peppers, green onion, vinegar, and garlic salt. Slice tops off rolls; scoop out centers. Fill rolls with cheese mixture; replace tops. Wrap rolls in foil. Heat at 400° for 15 to 20 minutes. Serve with mixed pickles and additional ripe olives, if desired. Makes 6 sandwiches.

Asparagus Cheesewiches

1 3-ounce package cream cheese,
    softened
  Dash garlic salt
  Dash dried oregano, crushed
2 English muffins, halved and toasted
1 tomato, peeled and cut in 4 slices
1 15-ounce can asparagus spears,
    drained
4 slices sharp American cheese
1 hard-cooked egg, sliced

Combine cream cheese, garlic salt, oregano, and dash pepper; spread evenly on muffin halves. Place in a 13x9x2-inch baking pan. Top each with a tomato slice and 3 or 4 asparagus spears. Cover pan with foil. Bake at 375° for 25 minutes. Uncover and top with cheese slices. Return to oven till cheese is melted, 2 to 3 minutes more. Garnish with hard-cooked egg slices. Makes 4 servings.

Gruyère-Apple Sandwiches

Thinly slice 4 triangles Gruyère cheese *or* 4 ounces Monterey Jack cheese into strips and place on 4 slices white bread. Core and slice 2 medium apples. Arrange apple slices on cheese; sprinkle with lemon juice. Top with 4 additional slices white bread. Spread softened margarine on the outside of sandwiches, top and bottom. Brown slowly on both sides in skillet or on griddle, 3 to 5 minutes on each side. Serve hot. Makes 4.

Cheese Buns Deluxe

1 cup shredded American cheese
⅓ cup chopped pitted ripe olives
¼ cup salad dressing or mayonnaise
2 tablespoons finely chopped celery
2 tablespoons chopped green onion
½ teaspoon curry powder
4 hamburger buns, split and toasted

Combine first 6 ingredients; mix well. Spread on toasted bun halves. Broil 4 inches from heat till cheese is bubbly, 1½ to 2 minutes. Makes 8 open-face sandwiches.

Peanut Butter Plus Sandwiches

8 slices white bread
  Margarine or butter, softened
½ cup peanut butter
¼ cup raisins
¼ cup orange marmalade

Spread bread slices with softened margarine. Spread *4 slices* of the bread with peanut butter. Sprinkle with raisins. Spread marmalade on remaining bread; place, marmalade-side-down, atop peanut butter. Makes 4.
  Variations: If desired, top peanut butter with a mixture of chopped celery and apple butter or a mixture of snipped dates and marshmallow creme.

Bayou Bean Burgers

1 15½-ounce can red kidney beans
¾ cup shredded sharp American cheese
¼ cup sweet pickle relish
¼ cup finely chopped onion
¼ cup salad dressing or mayonnaise
1 tablespoon prepared mustard
8 hamburger buns, split and toasted
  Margarine or butter, softened

Drain beans. Mix beans, ¼ *cup* cheese, relish, onion, salad dressing, and mustard. Spread buns with margarine. Spread ¼ cup bean mixture on bottom half of buns. Top with remaining cheese and bun tops. Wrap in foil. Heat at 350° for 20 minutes. Makes 8.

Create a cheese sandwich

Need an easy main dish? Don't forget the longtime favorite, toasted cheese. It is low cost as well as nutritious. For a change of pace, add tomato or hard-cooked egg slices, or try Swiss, Muenster, or Monterey Jack cheese instead of American cheese. As an extra touch, dip the sandwich in beaten egg and then in crushed potato chips before grilling.

Omelet Loaf

1 loaf French bread, halved lengthwise
¼ cup margarine, softened
4 ounces Monterey Jack cheese, sliced
    and cut in triangles
6 beaten eggs
1 cup diced tomato
1 3-ounce can chopped mushrooms,
    drained
½ cup evaporated milk
¼ cup sliced green onion
½ teaspoon salt
⅛ teaspoon pepper
2 tablespoons margarine or butter

Scoop out center of bottom half of bread; leave a 1-inch shell. Spread both halves with ¼ cup margarine; toast under broiler. Arrange cheese on bottom half. Combine next 7 ingredients. In skillet melt remaining margarine; add egg mixture. Cook over low heat till set, 5 to 8 minutes, folding over so uncooked egg goes to bottom. Spoon over cheese; replace top of bread. Slice. Serves 6.

Olive-Tuna Salad

1 6½- or 7-ounce can tuna, drained
    and flaked
1 cup sliced celery
1 hard-cooked egg, chopped
¼ cup chopped green pepper
2 tablespoons chopped pitted ripe
    olives
⅓ cup salad dressing or mayonnaise
1 teaspoon lemon juice
½ teaspoon Worcestershire sauce
¼ cup shredded American cheese
¾ cup crushed bite-size shredded
    rice squares
1 tablespoon margarine, melted

Combine first 5 ingredients. In small bowl combine salad dressing, lemon juice, Worcestershire, and ⅛ teaspoon salt. Fold into tuna mixture. Spoon into 4 greased and floured 6-ounce custard cups. Sprinkle each with 1 tablespoon cheese. Combine shredded rice squares and margarine. Spoon over cheese. Bake at 350° for 20 minutes. Serves 4.

Tuna-Gumbo Salad

1 10½-ounce can condensed chicken
    gumbo soup
¼ cup water
1 3-ounce package lemon-flavored
    gelatin
¼ cup salad dressing or mayonnaise
1 tablespoon vinegar
1 6½- or 7-ounce can tuna, drained
    and flaked
¼ cup diced celery
1 tablespoon snipped parsley
½ cup evaporated milk
    Cherry tomatoes

Combine soup and water. Add gelatin; cook and stir till gelatin is dissolved. With an electric mixer beat in salad dressing and vinegar. Stir in tuna, celery, and parsley. Chill till partially set. Meanwhile, pour evaporated milk into freezer tray and freeze till edges are icy. Whip to stiff peaks; fold into gelatin mixture. Pour into a 5-cup ring mold. Chill till firm. To serve, unmold salad and fill center with tomatoes. Makes 6 servings.

Tuna and Cheese Potato Salad

2 medium potatoes
2 tablespoons Italian salad
    dressing
1 tablespoon snipped parsley
5 cups torn lettuce
1 9¼-ounce can tuna, drained and flaked
3 hard-cooked eggs, quartered
3 ounces Swiss cheese, cut in strips
½ cup sliced pitted ripe olives
2 tablespoons finely chopped onion
• • •
½ cup Italian salad dressing

Cook potatoes in boiling salted water till tender, 25 to 35 minutes. Drain potatoes; peel and cube. Place potatoes in salad bowl; sprinkle with 2 tablespoons Italian dressing and the parsley. Layer lettuce, tuna, hard-cooked eggs, Swiss cheese, olives, and onion atop potatoes. Chill. At serving time, pour the ½ cup Italian dressing over salad; toss gently to coat. Makes 8 servings.

Salmon Salad in Tomato Cups

    1 7¾-ounce can salmon, drained, bones
        and skin removed, and flaked
    1 tablespoon lemon juice
    6 hard-cooked eggs, chopped
    ⅓ cup chopped celery
    ⅓ cup salad dressing or mayonnaise
    2 tablespoons sweet pickle relish
    ½ teaspoon salt
    ½ teaspoon dried dillweed
      Dash pepper
    6 medium tomatoes
      Lettuce

Sprinkle salmon with lemon juice; mix with remaining ingredients *except* tomatoes and lettuce. Chill. Turn tomatoes stem end down. Cut each into 6 wedges, *cutting to, but not through* bottom; sprinkle cut surfaces with salt. Spread wedges apart; spoon in egg mixture. Serve on lettuce. Serves 6.

Cottage-Salmon Salad

    1 16-ounce can salmon, drained, bones
        and skin removed, and broken in
        chunks
    2 cups cubed cooked potatoes
    ½ cup sliced celery
    ½ cup shredded carrot
    ¼ cup chopped green onion with tops
    1 hard-cooked egg, chopped
    1 cup cream-style cottage cheese
    ½ cup salad dressing or mayonnaise
    2 tablespoons milk
    1 tablespoon vinegar
    1 teaspoon dried dillweed
    ¼ teaspoon salt

Mix first 6 ingredients. Blend together remaining ingredients and dash pepper; add to salmon mixture. Toss to coat. Chill. Serve on green pepper rings and trim with carrot curls and green pepper, if desired. Serves 6.

Plan a luncheon around *Cottage-Salmon Salad* served over green pepper rings. This combination of salmon, potatoes, celery, hard-cooked eggs, and cottage cheese will satisfy your hungriest guests.

Sardine-Onion Salad

Chill one 8-ounce can sardines in tomato sauce. In a large salad bowl arrange 1 large head lettuce, torn; 12 cherry tomatoes; 1 small onion, cut into thin rings; ½ cup sliced celery; and ¼ cup sliced pitted ripe olives. Arrange 3 sliced hard-cooked eggs and sardines on top of salad mixture. Toss gently with enough French salad dressing to lightly coat. Makes 6 servings.

Black-Eyed Susans

  8 hard-cooked eggs, chopped
½ cup chopped pitted ripe olives
⅓ cup chopped celery
¼ cup salad dressing or mayonnaise
  3 tablespoons prepared mustard
  2 tablespoons chopped green onion
½ teaspoon salt
  8 unsplit frankfurter buns
    Margarine or butter, softened
    Lettuce

Combine the first 7 ingredients. Chill. Hollow out buns to ½ inch from edges. Spread buns with margarine; line with lettuce. Fill with egg mixture. Makes 8 servings.

Cottage-Macaroni Salad

1½ cups elbow macaroni
  1 cup cubed American cheese (4 ounces)
  1 cup cream-style cottage cheese
  1 cup chopped seeded cucumber
  1 cup shredded carrot
  2 tablespoons sliced green onion
¾ cup salad dressing or mayonnaise
½ cup dairy sour cream
  2 tablespoons vinegar
    Dash bottled hot pepper sauce

Cook macaroni according to package directions; rinse with cold water and drain. Combine macaroni and next 5 ingredients. Blend salad dressing, sour cream, vinegar, hot pepper sauce, and ¾ teaspoon salt. Toss with macaroni mixture. Chill. (If mixture seems dry, stir in a little milk.) Serves 6.

Swiss-Spinach Salad

  3 cups torn spinach
  3 cups torn lettuce
  8 ounces Swiss cheese, cut
    in thin strips
  3 hard-cooked eggs, cut in wedges
½ medium cucumber, sliced
  2 tablespoons chopped green onion
        • • •
½ cup salad dressing or mayonnaise
  2 tablespoons honey
  1 tablespoon lemon juice
  1 teaspoon caraway seed
  2 large oranges, peeled and sliced

In salad bowl arrange spinach, lettuce, Swiss cheese, hard-cooked eggs, cucumber, and green onion. Combine salad dressing or mayonnaise, honey, lemon juice, and caraway seed. Pour over salad. Toss lightly to coat. Garnish with orange slices. Serves 6 to 8.

Main Dish Tomato Cups

  6 medium tomatoes, peeled
  1 3-ounce package lemon-flavored
    gelatin
  1 cup boiling water
  1 5-ounce jar cheese spread
    with pimiento
¼ cup salad dressing or mayonnaise
¼ cup cold water
  2 teaspoons vinegar
    Dash bottled hot pepper sauce
⅓ cup diced cucumber
⅓ cup diced celery
    Lettuce

Cut slice from top of tomatoes. Scoop out centers; reserve and finely chop ½ cup pulp. Invert tomatoes; drain well. Sprinkle insides with salt. Dissolve gelatin and ¼ teaspoon salt in the boiling water. Add cheese spread and salad dressing; beat with rotary beater till smooth. Stir in cold water, vinegar, and hot pepper sauce. Chill gelatin mixture till partially set. Fold in reserved ½ cup tomato pulp, cucumber, and celery. Spoon gelatin mixture into tomato cups. Chill till firm. Serve tomato on lettuce. Makes 6 servings.

Savory soups and chowders

Tuna-Tomato Chowder

½ cup chopped onion
½ cup chopped celery
1 clove garlic, minced
2 tablespoons cooking oil
1 6-ounce can tomato paste
¼ cup long grain rice
1 teaspoon sugar
1 bay leaf
¼ teaspoon dried basil, crushed
   Dash bottled hot pepper sauce
1 6½- or 7-ounce can tuna, drained and
   flaked

In large saucepan cook onion, celery, and garlic in cooking oil till onion and celery are tender but not brown. Stir in tomato paste, uncooked rice, sugar, bay leaf, basil, hot pepper sauce, 4 cups water, and 1 teaspoon salt. Bring to boiling. Reduce heat; simmer, covered, 30 minutes. Stir in tuna. Heat through. Remove bay leaf. Makes 4 servings.

Salmon Bisque

½ cup chopped onion
½ cup chopped celery
2 tablespoons margarine
3 tablespoons all-purpose
   flour
1 teaspoon dried dillweed
½ teaspoon salt
¼ teaspoon garlic salt
¼ teaspoon Worcestershire sauce
4 cups milk
1 16-ounce can salmon, drained, bones
   and skin removed, and flaked
1 tablespoon lemon juice

In saucepan cook onion and celery in margarine till tender. Blend in flour, dillweed, salt, garlic salt, Worcestershire, and ⅛ teaspoon pepper. Add milk. Cook and stir till thickened and bubbly. Stir in salmon and lemon juice. Heat through. Season to taste. Makes 5 or 6 servings.

Shrimp-Celery Bisque

1 cup chopped celery
1 cup diced potato
¼ cup chopped onion
1 4½-ounce can shrimp, drained
2 cups milk
2 tablespoons all-purpose flour
2 tablespoons margarine or butter

In saucepan combine first 3 ingredients, 1 cup water, ½ teaspoon salt, and dash pepper. Simmer, covered, till vegetables are tender, about 15 minutes; stir often. Coarsely chop shrimp. Blend milk into flour till smooth; stir into potato mixture with shrimp and margarine. Cook and stir till thickened and bubbly. Makes 4 servings.

Curried Clam Chowder

1 cup chopped onion
1 teaspoon curry powder
2 tablespoons margarine or butter
2 tablespoons all-purpose flour
3 medium potatoes, peeled and chopped
1 8-ounce can tomatoes, cut up
1 tablespoon Worcestershire sauce
1 teaspoon paprika
½ teaspoon dried thyme, crushed
2 7½-ounce cans minced clams

In large saucepan or Dutch oven cook onion and curry in margarine till onion is tender. Blend in flour; add next 5 ingredients, 6 cups water, and 2 teaspoons salt. Simmer, uncovered, till potatoes are tender, about 30 minutes. Add undrained clams; simmer 5 minutes more. Makes 8 to 10 servings.

Cold weather favorite

Delight your family by ladling up generous servings of steaming *Shrimp-Celery Chowder.* Keep canned shrimp on hand so you can make this tasty seafood-vegetable chowder frequently.

Macaroni-Oyster Chowder

1 12-ounce can frozen oysters, thawed
1 cup chopped carrot
1 cup chopped celery
⅓ cup chopped onion
1 cup small shell macaroni
4 cups milk
¼ cup snipped parsley
⅛ teaspoon ground sage
2 tablespoons all-purpose flour
¼ cup margarine or butter
    Oyster crackers

Drain liquid from oysters into large saucepan. Add carrot, celery, onion, 2½ cups water, and 2 teaspoons salt. Bring to boiling. Gradually add macaroni. Cook, covered, till macaroni is tender, 10 to 12 minutes. Stir in *3 cups* of the milk, parsley, sage, and ¼ teaspoon pepper. Blend remaining 1 cup milk into the flour; add to chowder. Cook and stir till thickened. Meanwhile, cook oysters in margarine till edges curl; stir into chowder. Serve with crackers. Makes 6 servings.

New England Fish Chowder

1 pound fresh or frozen fish fillets
4 cups cubed potatoes
2 cups water
1 cup chopped onion
½ cup diced carrot
1 teaspoon salt
¼ teaspoon pepper
2 cups milk
1 13-ounce can evaporated milk
2 tablespoons all-purpose flour
    Margarine or butter

Thaw frozen fish. Dice fish and set aside. In 4-quart Dutch oven combine potatoes, water, onion, carrot, salt, and pepper. Cover and bring to boiling. Reduce heat; simmer 10 minutes. Stir in diced fish; cook, covered, 10 minutes more. Stir *1½ cups* of the milk and the evaporated milk into fish mixture. Blend remaining milk into flour; stir into fish mixture. Cook and stir till thickened and bubbly. Season to taste. Serve in bowls; top with pats of margarine. Serves 8.

Halibut Chowder

1 pound fresh or frozen
    halibut fillets
    Boiling water
3 medium carrots,
    bias sliced
½ cup bias-sliced celery
½ cup water
¼ cup chopped onion
2 10½-ounce cans condensed New
    England-style clam chowder
2 cups milk
2 tablespoons chopped canned pimiento
2 tablespoons snipped parsley

Thaw frozen fish. In skillet cover halibut with boiling water. Cover; simmer till fish flakes easily, 5 to 10 minutes. Drain; break fillets into chunks. In 2-quart saucepan combine carrots, celery, ½ cup water, and onion. Cook, covered, till tender, 12 to 15 minutes. Add clam chowder, milk, pimiento, and cooked halibut. Heat through. Sprinkle with parsley before serving. Serves 4.

Fish and Cheese Soup

Try perch, haddock, or halibut in this soup—

1 pound fresh or frozen fish fillets
¼ cup finely chopped onion
¼ cup chopped carrot
¼ cup chopped celery
2 tablespoons margarine or butter,
    melted
¼ cup all-purpose flour
¼ teaspoon salt
    Dash paprika
3 cups milk
1 13¾-ounce can chicken broth
½ cup cubed American cheese

Thaw frozen fish. Cut fish into bite-size pieces. Cook onion, carrot, and celery in margarine or butter till tender. Blend in flour, salt, and paprika. Add milk and chicken broth all at once. Cook and stir till thickened and bubbly. Add fish; return to boiling. Reduce heat; cook, uncovered, and stir till fish flakes easily, 5 to 8 minutes. Stir in cheese till melted. Serves 6.

Dilly Potato Soup

    3 cups cubed potatoes
    1 10½-ounce can condensed chicken broth
    1 cup thinly sliced celery
    ½ cup chopped onion
    ½ cup finely chopped carrot
    2 tablespoons snipped parsley
    1 teaspoon salt
    ¼ teaspoon dried dillweed
    ⅛ teaspoon pepper
  3½ cups milk
    2 tablespoons margarine or butter
    1 tablespoon chopped canned pimiento
    ½ cup milk
    ¼ cup all-purpose flour

In 3-quart saucepan combine first 9 ingredients. Cover and simmer till vegetables are tender, about 25 minutes. Add the 3½ cups milk, margarine, and pimiento. Heat through. Blend the ½ cup milk into the flour; stir into soup. Cook and stir till slightly thickened and bubbly. Makes 8 servings.

Corn Chowder

Crisp crackers are the perfect accompaniment to this delicious chowder—

    5 slices bacon
    1 medium onion, thinly sliced and
        separated into rings
    2 medium potatoes, peeled and diced
    ½ cup water
    2 cups milk
    1 17-ounce can cream-style corn
    1 teaspoon salt
    Dash pepper
    Margarine or butter

In saucepan cook bacon till crisp. Drain bacon, reserving 3 tablespoons drippings. Crumble bacon and set aside. In same saucepan cook onion in reserved drippings till lightly browned. Add diced potatoes and water; cook over medium heat till potatoes are tender, 10 to 15 minutes. Stir in milk, cream-style corn, salt, and pepper; cook till heated through. Pour chowder into warmed soup bowls; top each serving with crumbled bacon and a pat of margarine or butter. Serves 4 or 5.

Asparagus-Cheese Soup

    1 10-ounce package frozen cut
        asparagus
    1 tablespoon margarine or
        butter
    2 teaspoons all-purpose flour
    Milk
    ¼ teaspoon salt
    2 or 3 drops bottled hot pepper
        sauce (optional)
    Dash pepper
    1 cup shredded American cheese

Cook the asparagus according to package directions. Drain; reserve liquid. In saucepan melt margarine or butter; blend in flour. Add enough milk to reserved cooking liquid to equal 2 cups. Pour all at once into flour mixture. Cook, stirring constantly, till thickened and bubbly. Add asparagus; salt; hot pepper sauce, if desired; and pepper. Mix well. Add cheese; heat stirring constantly, till melted. Makes 4 to 6 servings.

Cheesy Onion Soup

    1 cup finely chopped onion
    ¼ cup chopped green pepper
    2 tablespoons margarine or butter,
        melted
    3 tablespoons all-purpose flour
    ¼ teaspoon salt
    ¼ teaspoon celery salt
    ¼ teaspoon Worcestershire sauce
    Dash pepper
    4 cups milk
    2 cups shredded sharp American
        cheese (8 ounces)
    6 melba toast rounds
    Grated Parmesan cheese

In saucepan cook onion and green pepper in margarine or butter till tender but not brown. Blend in flour, salt, celery salt, Worcestershire, and pepper. Add milk all at once. Cook and stir till thickened and bubbly. Add shredded cheese; stir to melt. Sprinkle melba toast with Parmesan; broil just till cheese is lightly browned. Serve soup in bowls; float toast atop. Makes 6 servings.

INDEX

T-Z